BISHOP DESMO
—THE VOICE
CRYING IN THE WILDERNESS

General Series Editor's Note

THE EMERGING CHURCH series aims at fresh, positive and well-informed thought on some of the crucial issues for Christians today. The Church exists to do God's will in the real world and here some of its thinkers submit their ideas for renewal in spirituality, structures, worship and witness. They are not armchair critics but men and women who distil their experience and describe their vision for the Christian community, so that after thought and prayer, the Church may redirect its work for the sake of the Gospel in contemporary England. There is no time to lose. The history of prayer book reform, changes in the Church/State relationship and attitudes to reunion, shows that about fifty years is needed in Britain for such proposals to be translated into practice. Discussion of the emerging church of the twenty-first century is needed now.

An African bishop speaking to some English fellow Christians just before his country gained independence, said 'Remember, God is always ahead.' This conviction unites all these authors.

ALAN WEBSTER
Dean of St Paul's, London

Bishop Desmond Tutu
—the voice of one

CRYING IN THE
WILDERNESS

*A collection of his recent statements in the
struggle for justice in South Africa*

Introduced and Edited by

John Webster

Foreword by
The Most Reverend Trevor Huddleston, CR
Bishop of Mauritius

MOWBRAY
LONDON & OXFORD

Introduction and notes Copyright © John Webster 1982
Text Copyright © Desmond Tutu

ISBN 0–264–66827–8

First published 1982
by A. R. Mowbray & Co. Ltd
Saint Thomas House, Becket Street
Oxford, OX1 1SJ

British Library Cataloguing in Publication Data

Tutu, Desmond
  Bishop Desmond Tutu: the voice of one
  crying in the wilderness.—
  (Mowbray's emerging
  church series)
  1. Blacks—South Africa—Segregation
  2. South Africa—Race relations
  I. Title   II. Webster, John
  261.7   BT734.3

ISBN 0-264-66827-8

Typeset in 'Monophoto' Times by Cotswold Typesetting Ltd, Gloucester
Printed in Great Britain by Richard Clay (The Chaucer Press), Bungay, Suffolk

'I am sorry to say that if no instructions had ever been addressed in political crises to the people of this country except to remember to hate violence, to love order, and to exercise patience, the liberties of this country would never have been attained.'

GLADSTONE

Foreword

I HAVE a very special reason for pride in writing the Foreword to this collection of Bishop Desmond Tutu's writings. As I have known him since he was a boy of thirteen and, in those now far off days had at least some part in encouraging him in his education, it is wonderful for me to see how he has become the voice of African hope and aspiration at this most dangerous time. It is even more wonderful that his voice has remained what it always was: a voice of Christian prophecy, compassion, and, perhaps surprisingly, Christian humour.

When I first knew him Bishop Desmond was ill with tuberculosis in a Johannesburg hospital and had to spend many weary months in bed. It is easy to recognize how difficult that must have been for one so full of energy and the joy of life. It was his own courage and patience that brought about his recovery and allowed him to complete his education so successfully. In his life as a priest, he has been to many countries and has had first-hand experience of the role of the Church throughout the world. He is therefore able to speak as a Black South African who, nevertheless, has seen Apartheid against a wide background and has known how it appears to those who live outside the racist ghetto created by the Government of South Africa.

The most remarkable quality of these writings is their heart-breaking charity towards those who persecute and attempt to destroy the very best people in South Africa. Bishop Desmond himself has had his passport confiscated twice in order to prevent him speaking freely outside his own country, and inside that country he is of course under constant surveillance. He has a passion for peace and reconciliation as being the expression of Christian love. But he recognizes, as all of us should but many do not, that Christian charity must be based on Justice. He also expresses that essential truth about the Christian Faith: that it is based on an infinite respect for human dignity and human rights because of the fact that God himself has taken human nature and

7

therefore endowed it with an infinite purpose and meaning which transcend the barriers of colour, race and creed.

Governments are always impossibly slow to recognize such truth and time is running out for peaceful solutions. The possibility of a blood bath in Southern Africa is horrifyingly real. If there is time, it is but a very short time. I can only hope and pray that this book will be widely read and that its message will be heard before it is too late.

> 'I tell you Naught for your Comfort
> Yea, Naught for your desire
> Save that the sky grows darker yet
> and the sea rises higher.'

A message that is still both a prophecy and a warning.

14 September 1981   TREVOR HUDDLESTON, CR

Contents

Foreword by The Most Reverend Trevor Huddleston, CR
      Bishop of Mauritius   *page* 7
Editor's Preface   11
Introduction by John Webster   13

PART ONE: THE EMERGING CHURCH

1   Jesus Christ—The Man for Others   27
2   The Church in the World   30
3   Politics and Religion   33
4   The Theology of Liberation   34

PART TWO: THE STRUGGLE FOR JUSTICE IN SOUTH AFRICA

5   Crisis and Response   39
6   The South African problem and Black Protest 40
7   Challenge and Invitation to White Students   42
8   To the White South African Community   44
9   To the South African Broadcasting Corporation 45
10 The South African Council of Churches—Our Work at
     the Grassroots   46
11 In Defence of the SACC   49
12 Where I Stand   52
13 Bishop Tutu's Testimony   55

PART THREE: WINDOWS INTO SOUTH AFRICA

14 Steve Biko—A Tribute   61
15 Robert Mangaliso Sobukwe   65
16 Polarisation   67
17 Banned People   68
18 Detention without Trial   69
19 Urban Unrest   70
20 Armed soldiers on routine police matters   71
21 A better approach   72
22 The Pass Laws   72

23 Christmas   74
24 Crossroads   74
25 R.14,000,000 and all that   76
26 Black Consciousness and Car Driving   78
27 A Message to Journalists   79
28 The Black Journalist and the Black Community   81
29 An Easter Message   82

PART FOUR: FREEDOM IS COMING

30 The Certainty of Freedom   87
31 The Black Mood Today   89
32 The Impact of the Soweto Riots   92
33 Free Nelson Mandela   94
34 Black Consumer Power—One lever for Change   97
35 My Vision for South Africa   99

PART FIVE: THE CHALLENGE OF THE EIGHTIES

36 Survival as a Human Society   105
37 Future Challenges: South Africa   106
38 The Affluent West and the Third World   111
39 A Prophetic Church and Human Rights in the Third
      World   113
40 Divided Churches   115
41 Women and the Church   119
42 Children's Rights   121
43 Into the Eighties   123

Bibliography   125

(A section of photographs appears between pages 64 and 65)

Editor's Preface

THIS COLLECTION of Bishop Tutu's sermons, speeches, articles and press statements documents a lively two-and-half years in the life of the South African Council of Churches, from Bishop Tutu's appointment as General Secretary on 1 March 1978, to the abortive meeting between the SACC and the South African Prime Minister and government in August 1980. The material is arranged so that Part One covers the general theoretical background, Part Two the practical work of the SACC, and Part Three the South African situation. Part Four deals with the forces of change in the country, and Part Five opens out into a look at the world, and the future role of the Church in it. A few of the pieces have been run together from several sources that all deal with the same subject; others have been extracted from a speech or address and reprinted under a sub-heading. Wherever possible the date has been given, and notes added to give the background and explain references.

I would like to thank everybody who has helped me with this book. Special thanks are due to the Revd Brian Brown, South Africa Secretary of the British Council of Churches, who has read and corrected the manuscript and made many valuable suggestions, as well as providing detailed information for the notes. I would like to thank Christian Journals Ltd of Belfast, for permission to quote Peter Matheson, and the Intermediate Technology Development Group for permission to quote from Marilyn Carr and George McRobie's paper. The books that I have consulted for information contained in the notes and introduction are listed in the bibliography. I would like to thank the staff of the USPG library, Westminister, for their help with research, and to Mowbray's Publishing Division for the consistent encouragement they have given. Finally I would like to thank my father, Alan Webster, who set this book in motion.

J.W.

Introduction

SOUTH AFRICA presents one of the most urgent challenges for the 1980s. The volcanic forces of African Nationalism cannot be held in check forever, and unless the Pretoria government dismantles the apartheid system, and accepts change gracefully, a bloody confrontation will always be on the cards. If racial war erupts, it will not confine itself to South Africa and the world ignores at its peril this possible trigger of a Third World War.

The 1970s saw white minority rule in South Africa coming under increasing pressure. Neighbouring states—Mozambique, Angola and Zimbabwe—all attained independence, so now South Africa has neighbours extremely hostile to white minority rule, and who feel a strong bond with their oppressed brothers and sisters across their borders. The blacks in South Africa, who form 80% of the population, yet own only 13% of the land, and who are systematically discriminated against, are disaffected and frustrated, angry that apartheid still continues while freedom from foreign domination has reached right across Africa. A black trade unionist in East London, speaking in a TV interview screened in Britain, gave expression to this frustration. 'We are awake, we are awake', he kept saying. 'We can see what they are doing to us, and we do not like it. They have been sucking our blood for centuries.'

It is small wonder that feelings are so strong: the Nationalist government has never given any form of peaceful protest against apartheid a chance. It has reacted to peaceful demonstrations with teargas and bullets, and it has ignored the voice and the aspirations of the black population. It has constructed a whole armoury of repressive laws, that have been strengthened since the Sharpeville massacre in 1960. The 90 Day Detention Act of 1963 was replaced by the 180 Day Act two years later. The Terrorism Act of 1967 allowed the police to detain suspects indefinitely, without any access to solicitors or courts. 1974 saw an amendment to the Riotous Assemblies Act, allowing any political meeting to be outlawed by the Minister of Justice. The Internal Security Act of

1976 was used to silence newspapers, individuals and organisations.

So it is hardly surprising that blacks have been leaving South Africa, to train in the arts of war in neighbouring countries. The Soweto riots of 16 June 1976, when thousands of schoolchildren marched against a decree ordering Afrikaans to be taught in schools, speeded up this exodus. The riots began when police shot a thirteen year old boy in the back. At least 500 young blacks were killed by the security forces, and for many young blacks this experience showed that the only viable language was the language of force. Now the young black militants are slipping back into Soweto, trained as urban guerillas, and prepared to strike at the government that hurts their people in so many ways.

Apartheid has been described by John Kane-Berman as a 'comprehensive and technologically sophisticated system, seeking continuing political and economic mastery of one race and class by another'.

The methods used to maintain this system in South Africa are legion.

Africans are required to possess a pass for lawful movement, which must be produced on demand. They are supposed to live outside the cities, travelling to maintain these affluent preserves of the white population. In 1976 there were a quarter of a million convictions for violations of the Pass Laws, and at the time of writing one third of South Africa's prison population is made up of Pass Law offenders. Obviously extremely costly to operate, the Pass Laws are nevertheless a cardinal point in the maintenance of white supremacy and continue to be enforced.

Africans have no freehold rights in 'white areas', the areas where all the money and employment are concentrated; they can only own property in the barren 'homelands'. Those who leave the 'homelands' to find work end up in huge illegal shanty towns like Crossroads. While black workers are required to live in townships near their place of work, their wives and children are deemed to be 'superfluous appendages', and have to live many miles away in the 'homelands'. Consequently, South Africa is the only country in the

14

world to have brought charges against people for 'illegally harbouring wives and children'.

Blacks are, moreover, paid much less than white workers; a black farm labourer is paid £10 per month.

The Churches have not stood still in their response to the situation in South Africa. In the 1950s Trevor Huddleston felt compelled to pronounce that, 'The Church sleeps on, though sometimes it talks in its sleep', in frustration at its lack of awareness about apartheid. But following the Sharpeville massacre in 1960, when 69 people were shot dead during a peaceful demonstration against the Pass Laws, Christian concern grew rapidly. At conferences in Uppsala and Notting Hill in the late 1960s, the World Council of Churches (WCC) decided on a more forthright policy to combat the situation. In 1970 Dr Eugene Carson Blake, the General Secretary of the WCC, visited South Africa, and shortly afterwards announced that they were making funds available to the liberation movements of Southern Africa, the African National Congress (ANC) and the Pan Africanist Congress (PAC), who had taken up the gun after Sharpeville.

Though these grants were not for arms, but for social services and medical supplies, the announcement of the WCC grant caused enormous controversy. Christian nations ever ready to sanctify their own wars suddenly became pacifist—as Bishop Tutu has pointed out many times. But the announcement of the grant was a bombshell for the South African Council of Churches. Though the SACC had not in fact been consulted over the grant, the Prime Minister, Mr Vorster, immediately threatened dire consequences if the SACC did not withdraw from the WCC. At the tense meeting that followed, they nevertheless decided to remain affiliated, but to repudiate the use of violence to bring about social change. 'People may not like where they stand, but they can do no other', commented Kairos, the journal of the SACC. The government reaction was to make it illegal for the Churches to send funds to the WCC, and to refuse entry visas to anyone connected with them.

The years 1960–71 had indeed been crucial for the Churches: they had come to assume a markedly independent position. The

time was ripe for a significant development within the Church—
the emergence, since the mid-1970s, of Bishop Desmond Tutu as
one of South Africa's most articulate Christians. Perhaps more
than any before him, Bishop Tutu has instilled in white Christians
an awareness of the hopes and aspirations of the black population.

Reaction from all quarters has shown him to be a difficult person
to ignore. His marked lack of hatred and desire for justice join
forces with an abundant sense of humour, and his evident concern
for good relations between the races confounds any attempt to
write off Desmond Tutu as a Communist or a terrorist. His South
African citizenship deprives the government of the final resort of
deportation—a tactic generally employed to deal with resolute
opponents of apartheid—Trevor Huddleston and Bishop
Ambrose Reeves, to name but two. So this courageously out-
spoken and effective opponent of apartheid continues to operate
openly in South Africa.

Since his appointment as General Secretary of the SACC, Tutu
has repeatedly challenged the blinkered thinking and repressive
policies of the Nationalist government, that destabilize the whole
of Southern Africa, ironically threatening the white community
with its own destruction. He has publicly confronted the government with the effects of aparteid on the black majority in Africa,
and spoken up forcefully for the oppressed. Under his leadership
the SACC has come to directly aid political prisoners, a
development that has inevitably infuriated white South Africans,
and indeed made many white Christians uneasy about the SACC's
work.

Bishop Tutu's work could be said to answer the particular
demands made of any preacher by the twentieth century: refusing
to confine himself to a church environment, he has spoken out in
many diverse situations, willingly using the press as a vehicle of
communication. This independence of mind and readiness to
tackle subjects not traditionally associated with the concerns of the
Church have proved a welcome intervention in the life of a
country which he aptly describes as 'claustrophobic'.

Desmond Tutu was born on 7 October 1931, in Klerksdorp, a

town in the Western Transvaal, seventy miles west of Johannesburg. His father was a Methodist schoolteacher, teaching in a primary school. Desmond was educated at a Swedish Mission boarding school at Roodeport, after which he attended a secondary school for blacks. In 1945, at the age of fourteen, he contracted tuberculosis, and spent twenty months in a Sophiatown hospital run by the fathers of the Community of the Resurrection. During his period of hospitalization he was visited once a week by Trevor Huddleston, then priest in charge of this black suburb of Johannesburg (now designated a 'white' area and renamed Triomf). Huddleston was already a respected opponent of apartheid, and became a source of inspiration for Tutu from this time onward; in later years, Desmond Tutu was to name his own son 'Trevor' in tribute to Huddleston, and the two men have remained firm friends.

After recovering from TB, he completed his studies in 1950, and went on to a teacher training college in Pretoria, where he spent three years. He had originally wanted to become a doctor, and had gained a place at medical college, but there was not enough money to pay the fees.

The next four years were spent teaching in Johannesburg and Krugersdorp, and during this period he married Leah, also a teacher, and a former pupil of his father. But when Dr Verwoerd introduced the Bantu Education Act, which took the education of black children out of the hands of the Church, and placed it into the hands of a negligent civil authority, Desmond Tutu decided he could 'have no truck with it', and subsequently decided to enter the ministry. He was accepted by Bishop Ambrose Reeves in 1957, and was made a deacon in the year of Sharpeville. He worked in the Benoni district of East Johannesburg, and was ordained in 1961. In 1962 he moved to England, and studied at Kings College, London. He remained in Britain till 1967, working in St Albans, and for the WCC. Back in South Africa, he worked in the diocese of Grahamstown, and from 1970-74 he was a lecturer at the University of Botswana, Lesotho, and Swaziland. He then spent another year in Britain, working in the diocese of Southwark.

On his return to South Africa in 1975, he was appointed Dean of Johannesburg, the first black person to be appointed to that post. He gained respect by taking up his residence in the township of Soweto, rather than moving into a more luxurious deanery in the 'whites only' section of Johannesburg. Following the Soweto riots of 16 June 1976, he rose to prominence as a commentator on the South African scene. In the same year he was made Bishop of Lesotho, but resigned this post one year later, in order to take up the post of General Secretary of the SACC. Bishop Tutu now had a prominent and representative position from which to work, and he used this to send out his clear calls for justice and social reform.

After a European tour in 1979, the government, stung by a statement calling on Denmark to boycott sales of South African coal, withdrew his passport in January 1980. This governmental action was condemned by the Archbishop of Canterbury and twenty-four bishops, in a statement which said, 'In our judgement, no satisfactory reason has been given, and since Bishop Tutu has been charged with no crime, the confiscation of his passport must be seen as a seriously disturbing harassment of the SACC. This we deplore, and earnestly request that the Bishop's passport be returned, to enable him to continue his ecumenical work.'

In May 1980, Bishop Tutu took part in a march in Johannesburg to protest at the arrest of the Revd John Thorne, the former General Secretary of the SACC. As the group of fifty-three marchers, which included thirty-five clergymen, approached John Vorster Square, they were met by soldiers in combat uniforms, carrying machine guns, and by a brigadier with a loudhailer. 'Reverends, you are under arrest', he informed them, and the entire contingent was promptly detained and taken to the police station in John Vorster Square. There they were fingerprinted, photographed 'for the rogues gallery', and put in the cells overnight, before appearing in court next morning. Bishop Tutu later described how, as the black ministers of religion from different churches were lumped together in one cell, they realized something of church unity, something they had been 'discussing for donkey's years'. In the morning, after a court appearance, the marchers were released, and later fined R.50 each.

Though Bishop Tutu commented later that the action of the authorities—'they don't know how to react to peaceful demonstrations'—gave this incident more attention than it was perhaps worthy of, he said that it established an important point. 'No longer are we going to be Churches that merely pass pious resolutions.' Bishop Tutu honours this in his day-to-day life: he refuses to carry a pass, carrying instead some other form of ID, like a driving license, or a passport, when it is not locked up in the Minister of Police's safe!

Bishop Tutu's passport was eventually restored in January 1981, but he did not retain it for long. Following another tour of Europe and the USA, in February and March 1981, his comments to the effect that the South African regime was the most vicious since the Nazis, provoked the same reaction—his passport was again confiscated on his return, a mere three months after its restoration.

The harassment of the SACC continues; on 22 June 1981 the SACC's director of Mission and Evangelism, the Revd Sol Jacobs, was arrested and detained. As Bishop Tutu puts it: 'It has sometimes seemed as if we were operating in a country behind the Iron Curtain.'

Bishop Tutu was in London in March 1981, and on hearing that Mr Botha (the South African Prime Minister) intended to confiscate his passport on the Bishop's return to South Africa, he gave a press conference at the Headquarters of the British Council of Churches. He was unrepentant: he was after all talking about peaceful change, and this attempt to muzzle him should at least make the world community realize the kind of obstacles encountered in any attempt to talk with those whose sole interest lies in clinging on to power. It was not a solemn occasion; even the serious-looking man from a South African newspaper smiled at the occasional comment. But there was an intensity too, that was revealed when he was asked about his attitude towards the insurgents in South Africa. 'I would like to throw this question back to the West', he insisted; how could people praise the French resistance, or (rightly) regard Dietrich Bonhoeffer as a hero for his attempted plot on Hitler's life, but suddenly become pacifist when blacks took up arms? Many of those fighting had been committed Christians, taking up the armed struggle as a last resort. The Afrikaners, the USA, and Britain had all fought in the cause of their freedom. However, Bishop Tutu, with South Africa 'half a minute to midnight', was still looking for a peaceful solution.

The whole problem of violence, and the more specific question of when its use could be justified in the cause of freedom from oppression, are perhaps irresolvable—until the situation demands that a choice be made. It cannot be denied that non-violent action to bring about social change can be extremely effective—as has been amply demonstrated by the lives and work of Gandhi and Martin Luther King: both men changed the face of their countries through non-violent means. Yet peaceful methods of attempting change are often seen as ineffective by the oppressed—a sense born of bitter experience. Bishop Tutu tells of a twelve-year-old boy saying to him, 'Father, show me what you have achieved with all your talk of peaceful change, and I will show you what we gained with just a little violence.'

The main opposition party in South Africa, the African National Congress (ANC), moved away from non-violent strategy in 1961, after the Sharpeville massacre. The aim of the ANC, formed in 1912, is to achieve a non-racial democracy in South Africa, based on the Freedom Charter signed in Kliptown in 1955. Their decision to set up an armed branch of their organization was not arrived at lightly. Since their formation, they had been committed to the techniques of non-violence that had been used by Gandhi himself in South Africa. In the aftermath of Sharpeville, however, ANC leaders, assessing the South African situation, came to the bleak realization that fifty years of non-violence had not brought the reality of a non-racial society any closer. On the contrary, their peaceful demands had been met with escalating force and increasingly repressive legislation. They felt it unrealistic to continue solely with non-violent strategy. While Bishop Tutu is himself working for a peaceful solution of the South African political problem, he feels bound to make the West aware that the freedom fighters have widespread support amongst the black population. 'The guerillas are our children, our brothers and our sisters', he was quoted as saying in the British press. The West should not see them in the same light as the Baader-Meinhof group, or the Red Brigades, because 'in their countries there are political institutions available to those who take up the gun. In South Africa there are none.'

Some Westerners see the ANC in terms of Soviet expansionism, and recently a new phrase has come into politics—'international terrorism'. This phrase, when applied to the genuine liberation movements of the world, clearly demonstrates the doublethink that Western nations suffer from in their attitudes towards violence. For so long the main movers in global politics, they now find it hard to accept that there are other actors on the stage. Moreover, many who use this term were strong supporters of the Vietnam war—a war which can quite reasonably be regarded as the greatest act of international terrorism in modern times.

The Churches in South Africa continue to hope that reason will prevail, and that the government and the white community will recognize black aspirations, and start to move the country towards a just solution. If this does not happen we will see a confrontation between the bully boys of the security forces, and the progressive forces in the country. It is in an effort to avoid this confrontation that Bishop Tutu and other black leaders are asking the West to exert more pressure on the Pretoria government, and so increase the chances of a negotiated settlement.

Yet Western nations and Western business interests continue to prop up aparteid in numerous ways. A large proportion of the armaments used in the illegal occupation of Namibia, and for murderous raids into the independent states of Mozambique and Angola, were made and supplied by the West prior to the 1977 UN arms embargo. The oil that fuels the apartheid war machine is still flowing into South Africa. She herself possesses no oil deposits, and an effective oil boycott would greatly increase the chances of bringing Pretoria to the negotiating table. Since 1973 African and

Arab oil producers have refused to sell to South Africa, but Western companies have not followed this lead, and currently supply 85% of South Africa's oil needs. Foreign investment plays its part in helping apartheid to exist. Total British investment in South Africa amounts to £7 billion, and European and US banks are strong contributors to the apartheid economy. Though the arms embargo of 1977 was agreed unanimously by the United Nations, subsequent attempts to impose economic sanctions on South Africa, in 1980 and 1981, were vetoed by Britain, France and the USA.

If the West wishes to see a democracy in South Africa, it *must* use the ample means at its disposal to answer Bishop Tutu's call.

When one thinks of the role the Church has not infrequently played in society in the past—a role that has led to excesses of the order of the Crusades and the Inquisition—it is good to see a section of the Church identifying with the poor and oppressed, and willing to speak up for those without a voice. The experiences of Bishop Tutu, as documented here, point in a new and hopeful direction, with implications beyond South Africa.

Tutu's description of the white South African, checking his burglar alarms and his watch dogs, is all too relevant to the renewed world-wide militarisation currently turning our planet into an armed camp. The white South African knows in his heart that true security consists in a population whose members are contented, because all share equitably in the good things of life. Similarly, justice and equality are the touchstones of world peace.

Another important element in Bishop Tutu's teaching is the emphasis he places on human power and potential. So many people are repelled by a view of humanity that seems joyless and depressing, and it is remarkable that though Bishop Tutu works in a situation where apartheid reveals the selfish and destructive aspects of humanity, he still takes a positive attitude towards people.

There is much to be learned from Bishop Tutu's experiences in South Africa. His approach has a cutting edge that integrates

22

religion with the issues of the day. He gives hope to people, and communicates the feelings of the oppressed to those in power. He also believes that peace and reconciliation are possible through this open, honest communication, no matter what the social pressures are to keep quiet. Through his work, and that of the South African Council of Churches, we can get a glimpse of a Church independent from the State, working for peace and justice, and making a real and welcome contribution to our world.

September 1981   JOHN WEBSTER

SOUTHERN AFRICA

Part One

The Emerging Church

1. Jesus Christ—The Man for Others

From the Churches of the Third World, so often confronted with massive problems of poverty and injustice, comes an earthier, grittier view of Christ, and a forthright attitude towards the role of the Church in society. This section has been taken from sermons preached by Bishop Tutu in the Cathedrals of Johannesburg, Maritzburg and New York.

THE GOD whom we worship is wonderfully transcendent—St John in his Gospel sums it all up by saying 'God is Spirit'. Yet when this God wanted to intervene decisively in the affairs of Man, he did not come as a spiritual being. He did not come as an angel. No, he became a human being. He came in a really human and physical way—his mother became pregnant, and he was born as a helpless baby, depending on mother and father for protection, for food, for love and for teaching. When they looked for him in the houses of Kings and the high and mighty, he was born in a stable, as one of the lowly and despised. He worked as the village carpenter, knowing what it meant for a mother to lose her only coin, to sweep out the house diligently by candlelight, until she found the lost coin and rejoiced at the finding.

If we could go back to the days when our Lord walked here on earth and we asked people: 'What sort of person is this Jesus?' we would get many different answers. Some would say 'Oh, he tells such beautiful but funny stories—he really is a powerful creature.' Or, 'He is very brave—he is not afraid of the rulers.' But I am sure most people would say: 'Really, I have never seen anyone who cares so much for people, especially people in trouble. He cared for us when we were in the wilderness and we were hungry. God gave him the power to multiply the bread and fishes and he fed us. His disciples had said he should send us away hungry and he had refused.' Nowhere are we told that he ever turned anybody away who was in need; no matter how busy he was he never neglected anybody.

There is nothing that might be called otherworldly about this ministry of Jesus. He scandalised the religious leaders of his day, the prim and proper ones, because he consorted with the social and religious pariahs of his day. The religious establishment saw him as a young upstart who had no religious training, who had not sat at the feet of any renowned rabbi. What was more, he came to turn upside down everything they knew. He came sowing all kinds of confusion. He had dared to have dinner with Zaccheus, a tax collector, a collaborator with the Roman oppressor, and had had the temerity to call him the son of Abraham. He had invited another tax collector, Levi, to become one of his special followers. He had gone to dinner in his house, and there, quite horribly, incredibly, He had sat at the table with all the riff-raff of the town, those whom every respectable person would not be seen dead with, let alone supping with them—those prostitutes, those sinners, those drug addicts, the so-called scum of society. Moreover, when the establishment men, the Pharisees and the Saducess, those who knew everything about God and religion, when they challenged him, He was not in the least bit embarassed. No, he said: 'Only the sick need a doctor, not those who are well.' He said he had come to find those who were lost. He even said, quite unbelievably, that these prostitutes, these sinners, would precede the religious teachers and leaders into Heaven. Jesus revolutionised religion by showing that God was really a disreputable God, a God on the side of the social pariahs. He showed God as one who accepted us sinners unconditionally.

We could not accuse our Lord of using religion as a form of escapism from the harsh realities of life, as most people live and experience it. The jibe of the Marxist could not apply to him—he never used religion as an opiate of the people, promising them 'pie in the sky when you die'. He knew that people want their pie here and now, and not in some future tomorrow. A postmortem pie is an oddity in any case. No, for he described in the parable of the last judgement what makes us fit or unfit for Heaven, and those criteria have nothing that you could call religious or otherworldly, in the narrow sense, about them. We qualify ourselves for Heaven by whether we have fed the hungry, clothed the naked, visited the sick or those imprisoned. And Jesus said to do these things to the least of his brethren, is to have done them as to him.

We need to remind ourselves constantly that Jesus was heir to the prophetic tradition. You cannot read any of the major prophets without being struck by at least one thing. They all condemned, as worthless religiosity, a concern with offering God worship when we were unmindful of the socio-political implications of our religion. Such worship and religion they condemned roundly as quite unacceptable to God, and for that reason an abomination and worthless. For Jesus, as for them, all of Life belongs as a whole to God, both in its secular and sacred aspects. They could not have understood our peculiar habit of compartmentalising Life, and nor could Jesus.

Listen to Isaiah 58. 1–8; the same words can be echoed by other prophets.

The Lord says, 'Shout as loud as you can! Tell my people Israel about their sins! They worship me every day, claiming that they are eager to know my ways, and obey my laws. They say that they want me to give them just laws, and that they take pleasure in worshipping me.'

The people ask, 'Why should we fast if the Lord never notices? Why should we go without food if he pays no attention?'

The Lord says to them, 'The truth is that at the same time as you fast, you pursue your own interests and oppress your workers. Your fasting makes you violent, and you quarrel and fight. Do you think this kind of fasting will make me listen to your prayers? When you fast you make yourselves suffer; you bow your heads low like a blade of grass, and you spread out sackcloth and ashes to lie on. Is that what you call fasting? Do you think I will be pleased with that?

The kind of fasting I want is this: remove the chains of oppression, and the yoke of injustice, and let the oppressed go free. Share your food with the hungry, and open your homes to

29

the homeless poor. Give clothes to those who have nothing to wear, and do not refuse to help your own relatives.

Then my favour will shine on you like the morning sun, and your wounds will be quickly healed. I will always be with you to save you; my presence will protect you on every side.'

Jesus believed that he was fighting against the evil one on behalf of God to establish God's Kingdom. Suffering, hunger, disease, poverty—all these things were the result of evil. He spoke of disease sometimes as bondage—Satan had enslaved the sick person, because he did not like us to be free. And Jesus came to bring wholeness and healing where there was disease.

An equally important truth about Jesus was that he was a man of prayer, a man of God. It was the intimate communion with his Father which formed his life's blood. Thus we can understand his cry of dereliction and anguish, 'My God, My God, why has thou forsaken me?', when our sins blotted out for him his experience of God the Father. Prayer, and communion with the Father were like breathing to him. We see him going into a forty-day retreat, to learn about the nature of his vocation as a Messiah. Prayer and spirituality were central in the life of our Lord, and he was the man for others only because first and foremost he had been the man of God.

2. The Church in the World

Taken from an address given in Pretoria at the Presbyterian Church Assembly, and from a sermon preached at St Cyprians Church in Sharpeville.

THIS TWOFOLD movement or pattern in our Lord's life must be ours as well. We cannot use religion as a form of escapism, skulking behind our prayers, because that cannot be an authentic Christian spirituality. Equally we cannot engage in a merely worldly 'busyness' or activism. For then what do we bring that is distinctive to the hectic business of sorting out our problems?

The Church of God has to be the salt and light of the world. We are the hope of the hopeless, through the power of God. We must transfigure a situation of hate and suspicion, of brokenness and separation, of fear and bitterness. We have no option. We are servants of the God who reigns and cares. He wants us to be the alternative society; where there is harshness and insensitivity, we must be compassionate and caring; where people are statistics, we must show they count as being of immense value to God; where there is grasping and selfishness, we must be a sharing community now.

In the early Church people were attracted to it not so much by the preaching, but by the fact that they saw Christians as a community, living a new life as if what God had done was important, and had made a difference. They saw a community of those who, whether poor or rich, male or female, free or slave, young or old—all quite unbelievably loved and cared for each other. It was the lifestyle of the Christians that was witnessing.

We witness too, by being a community of reconciliation, a forgiving community of the forgiven. We need it in the world today, don't we? But how can we say we offer the remedy to the world's hatreds and divisions, if we ourselves as Christians are divided into different churches, if we are unforgiving, if we don't greet or speak to certain people? People will be right to say 'Physician heal thyself!' We must not only speak about forgiveness and reconciliation—we must act on these principles.

We must witness by service to others, by being their servants in all sorts of ways. In our country, South Africa, the Church must be there in the poverty and squalor, to bring the love and compassion of God amongst the sick, the hungry, the lepers, the disabled and the naked. We must proclaim that in a country of injustice and oppression, where Blacks receive an inferior education, are forced to live in matchbox houses, cannot move freely from place to place, and have to leave their wives and families behind when they want to work in town—we must declare that this is God's world. He is on the side of the oppressed, of the poor, of the despised ones. We must say these things even if they make us suffer. It is not politics. It is the Gospel of Jesus Christ the liberator who will set us free. In this country those who say these things are detained without trial, as your new rector was. They are banned, they are threatened with death, as your Minister was. But we cannot keep quiet, because if we kept quiet then the very stones would cry out. When they knew Bishop Tutu was coming to preach here today [*at St Cyprians, Sharpeville*] then the Special Branch came. You saw them as we were processing around the township—sitting in their cars to watch the Church of God. Let us be the Church of God, fearlessly proclaiming his Gospel.

The identification with the poor is a costly business. It leads to vilification and ostracism. Christ not only suffered but was eventually killed for it. If the Church is a serving Church, it will be a suffering Church as well. Suffering is a hard fact of reality, and human beings have, down the ages, tried to make sense of what appeared to be so meaningless. The dualists claimed there were two eternal principles: a God of goodness, light and spirit, who was in conflict with a God of evil, darkness and matter. Suffering occurred because our world was the arena for this conflict.

The Hindu or Buddhist deal with suffering by saying it doesn't really exist—it is all illusion. Unfortunately someone with an excruciating toothache does not find much relief in being told it is illusory. Another view that has been influential down the ages is the one that says: 'You suffer because you are a sinner.' However, Jesus repudiated this view: when confronted with a man born blind and asked whether he or his parents had sinned, he responded that neither had sinned.

The breakthrough in Biblical teaching came when suffering could be seen as redemptive, and not merely wasteful. This teaching was fulfilled in Jesus Christ. He suffered and died for us, overcoming suffering and making available to us the same power. While on earth he did all he could to alleviate want, pain and anguish, yet he knew he had to suffer. It is of the essence of

Christianity, because He said, 'Unless you take up your cross and follow me, you cannot be my disciple.' An affluent, comfortable Church cannot be the Church of Christ—an affluent Church which uses its wealth for itself.

We must do all we can to alleviate suffering; there is so much to be done in this South Africa of plenty and affluence, where there is malnutrition, families sleeping on pavements, after being evicted from a house that stands empty behind them, just because they are the wrong colour. But having done all, there will still be suffering which remains for us a mystery. We know that our God is not an aloof, unmoved God. He came into our human existence, he knows it from inside and is touched by our anguish.

3. Politics and Religion

From an article in Kairos, the journal of the South African Council of Churches, 23 October 1978

IT IS interesting that when a religious leader should support a particular political system he is hardly ever accused of dabbling in politics. But woe betide the religious leader when he has the temerity to criticise a particular political status quo. He then runs the gauntlet of harsh criticism—for being a political predikant. For us it is not politics that determines our attitudes and actions. It is quite firmly our Christian faith which determines our socio-political involvement. We ask: is such and such an action, policy or attitude consonant with our understanding of the teachings of Jesus Christ? How does it square up to what He called the summary of the Law—loving God and loving ones neighbour; the two sides of the same coin.

So the Christian must always be critical of all political systems, always testing them against Gospel standards. Does this system usurp the place of God? Does the State require an absolute loyalty, a loyalty that deifies it? The State should be obeyed when it remains in its legitimate authority, but there are circumstances when it forfeits the allegiance of its subjects. The Christian's ultimate loyalty and obedience are to God, not to a movement or a cause, or a political system. If certain laws are not in line with the imperatives of the Gospel then the Christian must agitate for their repeal by all peaceful means.

Christianity can never be a merely personal matter. It has public consequences and we must make public choices. Many people think Christians should be neutral, or that the Church must be neutral. But in a situation of injustice and oppression such as we have in South Africa, not to choose to oppose, is in fact to have chosen to side with the powerful, with the exploiter, with the oppressor.

4. The Theology of Liberation

The growing influence of liberation theology in the deprived areas of the world, and its concern for the material as well as the spiritual welfare of the people, is reflected in this passage, taken from an address given in Pretoria, to the Presbyterian Church Assembly on 18 September 1978. Liberation theology offers an important opportunity for Christian renewal; as Peter Matheson says in Profile of Love*: 'The emergence of Liberation theology may yet prove to be the most creative Christian political initiative since Puritanism in the seventeenth century.'*

IN THE recent past, it used to be taken for granted that when you talked about Christian theology, then you were really referring to theology as it had been done or was being done in the great centres of Christianity in Western Christendom. You would be thought to be discussing theology as it was being written, taught or discussed

34

in the UK, North America or on the European Continent, especially in Germany. If you came from a Third World country, you would be expected to study the theologians produced in these great centres, if you yourself aspired to be a theologian who wanted to be taken account of in the future!

But we note that some of the best theologies have come not from the undisturbed peace of a don's study, or his speculations in a university seminar, but from a situation where they have been hammered out on the anvil of adversity, in the heat of battle, or soon thereafter. For too long Western theology has wanted to lay claim to a university that it cannot too easily call its own. Christians have found that the answers they possessed, were answers to questions that nobody in different situations was asking. New theologies have arisen, addressing themselves to the issues in front of them. Consequently we have in our midst now the theology of Liberation, as developed in Latin America, and Black theology, developed in the USA and Southern Africa.

The perplexity they have to deal with is this: Why does suffering single out black people so conspicuously, suffering not at the hands of pagans or other unbelievers, but at the hands of white fellow Christians who claim allegiance to the same Lord and Master?

A few years ago it became fashionable to say that the world sets the agenda for the Church. This represented a salutary shift of emphasis away from our unhealthy otherworldliness. Christians had wanted to shut themselves in a holy ghetto, almost entirely unmindful of the cries of the hungry, and the anguish of the poor and exploited ones of this world. There was an almost Manichean dread of the material, existent world, and Christians had to deny in an absolute way the world, the flesh and the devil—in order to concentrate on the world to come. Those who reacted against this unsatisfactory state of affairs declaimed approvingly that 'God loved not the Church, but the world'. Such a reminder was important; it represented a positive gain and we must give thanks that it happened. And yet one has the suspicion that the pendulum of reaction might just have swung too far, and that (to change the image) the baby has been thrown out with the bath water. What I

35

am trying to underline is that we cannot denigrate the Church, and devalue it, because we want to enhance the value of the world.

In South Africa, to refer now to some specifics, the Church of God must sustain the hope of a people who have been tempted to grow despondent, because the powers of this world seem to be rampant. It does not appear that significant political change can happen without much bloodshed and violence, and it seems that God does not care, or is impotent. The Church of God must say that despite all appearances to the contrary, this is God's world. He cares and cares enormously, his is ultimately a moral universe that we inhabit, and that right and wrong matter, and that the resurrection of Jesus Christ proclaims that right will prevail. Goodness and Love, Justice and Peace are not illusory, or mirages that forever elude our grasp. We must say that Jesus Christ has inaugurated the Kingdom of God, which is a Kingdom of Justice, Peace and Love, or fulness of life, that God is on the side of the oppressed, the marginalised and the exploited. He is a God of the poor, of the hungry, of the naked, with whom the Church identifies and has solidarity. The Church in South Africa must be the prophetic Church, which cries out 'Thus saith the Lord', speaking up against injustice and violence, against oppression and exploitation, against all that dehumanises God's children and makes them less than what God intended them to be.

Part Two

The Struggle for Justice in
South Africa

5. Crisis and Response

From an article entitled 'South Africa in crisis and our response as the children of God'.

THE SOUTH AFRICAN Council of Churches (SACC) has issued serious warnings that unless fundamental change occurs in the Republic reasonably quickly, then those who are working for peaceful change will rapidly become discredited. Many people, in desperation, will want to use violence as a last desperate resort. At this stage we in the SACC are still striving for a peaceful solution of the crisis in our land. But time is not on our side. Something must be done, and done urgently.

But a time of crisis is not just a time of anxiety and worry. It gives a chance, an opportunity, to choose well or to choose badly. You have to decide which way you want to go. It is possible in our country to choose the path that leads to a new and more open society—a society that is more just, where people matter because they were created in the image of God. Equally it is possible to choose the road that leads to our destruction, because it is the road of injustice and oppression. And we believe that unless we have real change in this beloved land, then we are going to have a bloodbath.

We want to avert that awful alternative. We in the SACC are committed to work for justice and peace! We are committed to reconciliation. We believe that the Churches can demonstrate the kind of society we are working for—a caring and compassionate society, where you count because you are a human being, and not because of your colour or your race. Some of this is already happening in a few of our churches. In St Mary's Cathedral in Johannesburg, black and white worship together under the leadership of a black Dean. In the SACC we have a staff of all races, black, white and brown, and all work harmoniously together. It can happen in the whole of South Africa. Please let us move away from the edge of the precipice. God is giving us perhaps our last chance.

6. The South African problem and Black Protest

From an address given at the University of Witwatersrand. (See following note.)

THE PROBLEM in South Africa is to do with political power as between white and black. When the Afrikaners came to power in 1948 they created laws, or reinforced others, which increased the total unacceptability for blacks of white minority rule. Nobody, or relatively few amongst the whites, are as opposed to white minority rule, as they are to so-called black majority rule. I believe in majority rule, not *black* majority rule. That is what democracy is about, and dear vilified former terrorist Mugabe, now Prime Minister *Mr* Mugabe, has shown what blacks can do, and how magnanimous they are. He is no racist.

Blacks execrated, and still execrate with their whole beings the system of white minority rule. They are pledged to see it changed or destroyed. They have protested since the beginning of this century, against the gross injustices and inequities they have experienced. They have gone on delegations overseas; they have waited on governments in South Africa; they have signed petitions; they have staged protest marches; they have appealed for justice and fairness, and for the removal of structural violence. They have protested against low pay and the pass laws, they have participated in puppet impotent bodies set up by the government, in the hope that their willingness to co-operate would demonstrate their earnestness to the government, and thus elicit greater understanding of their plight. It has all, it appears, been in vain. The best organised and most widespread protest in which blacks participated, was the passive resistance campaign of the 1950s, when black people deliberately broke immoral and discriminatory laws. In many ways this led to the protests against the Pass Laws, which culminated in the Sharpeville killings of 21 March 1960. The world

40

was appalled that blacks, protesting peacefully, could be mowed down so ruthlessly; many were shot in the back, and there was never any question of the police being in danger.

That is part of our history, etched forever into our memories, and burning itself into black psyches. Following the pattern shown in the Afrikaner resistance movement (against the British), there has been an escalation in the black protest movement. There has been a disengagement following the failure of appeals and verbal protests. We have seen the disengagement from white contact through the Black Consciousness movement—a movement absolutely crucial to true reconciliation.

And so we came to the Soweto riots of June 1976. Afrikaners, who had fought against English being imposed on them, in their turn wanted to impose Afrikaans upon the blacks, who rightly or wrongly, regard it as the language of the oppressor. There was an explosion South Africa had not been prepared for, not even the police, who had riddled our society with despicable creatures called informers. After 16 June 1976 our white fellow South Africans were frightened. They thought Armageddon had arrived. Gun shops were emptied of their stock.

Afrikaans was a symbol of a whole system of oppression, injustice and exploitation. Cheap labour, the destruction of black family life, overcrowded trains and buses, small matchbox houses in dreary smog-filled townships, (which lack the most elementary amenities which other sections of the community take for granted), a system of education deliberately inferior to that of the other communities—all these and more were symbolised by the Afrikaans issue. So South Africa went up in flames.

But even now nothing much has changed. Black anger is growing. Blacks are being endorsed out even more stringently, and dumped anywhere, as long as they are out of sight and so out of mind. They are starving in a country that boasts of sending food to Zambia, to starve as part of the solution of the South African political crisis, the so-called solution which is that there will be no black South Africans.

Thus many blacks have said: 'We give up. We have tried

everything peaceful and we have failed. Our last resort is to fight for the right to be human, for the right to be a South African.' And so South Africa faces the prospect of a civil war again. The Voortrekkers protested, then disengaged, then fought. Blacks have protested, have disengaged, and some of them are now fighting. Whites have boys on the border; blacks have boys on the other side.

What we say is: there is probably just time for a reasonably peaceful resolution of our crisis. We are still crying out that we are committed to justice, reconciliation and peace. We are still holding out our hands of fellowship, and saying to our white compatriots 'grasp them—let us talk while there is still time. If we can solve our crisis then we have as South Africans, black and white together, a tremendous contribution to make to Africa and the rest of the world. God has blessed us with a wonderful country, large enough to accommodate and support all of us, black and white, most comfortably.'

If the government however, is determined to balkanise South Africa, and snatch away citizenship from blacks, then there will not be a peaceful solution, for they are declaring war on us. What are blacks then expected to do in such a situation? Fold their hands?

7. Challenge and Invitation to White Students

While an increasing number of students are becoming involved in the struggle for social change, many are still content to accept their unjust privileges. This challenge to them, with the preceding analysis of the South African situation, was delivered to an audience of students at Witwatersrand University, on 18 March 1980, at a meeting of the Student Representative Council's Academic Freedom Committee.

Is THIS present South Africa what you want for your children, a divided segregated South Africa where there is freedom for no one really? *You* suffer also because of discrimination, you are diminished because you can't have as a neighbour anyone you want. Your choices are limited—you have to marry into certain races which are determined for you. You can't discuss openly and freely. What do you really know about Communism or Marxism? You are brainwashed by the South African Broadcasting Corporation (SABC) which constantly misleads you, as it does its propaganda work for the Nationalist party. And you just sit around and do nothing about it.

In your name various people are banned, even after fifteen years on Robben Island. They come out of prison, where they could hardly be said to have engaged in subversive activities, only to be banned for another five years, to be prisoners at their own expense. You sit around and do nothing about it, you say nothing about it. You are too busy getting your degrees, so that you can be qualified to enter the rat-race. But all these actions are done in your name, and in the name of Christian civilisation and free enterprise. In your name people are locked up in detention barracks because they are opposed to all wars as pacifists. You accept it all quite comfortably. You sleep in your white sheets after a sumptuous meal, and you say and do nothing about a government which refuses people the right of conscientious objection. South Africa is the only country in the so-called free world which denies the right of conscientious objection. A priest is given a vicious sentence for attending a Church conference and you say and do nothing about it. Blacks are moved like so many cattle from place to place, to preserve your identity and your privilege, and you go on as if nothing untoward had occurred. *All these diabolical schemes occur in your name.* Even after the Sharpeville massacre, the Soweto riots, you seem quite content to have it so, for you say and do virtually nothing.

We are committed to black liberation, because thereby we are committed to white liberation. You will never be free until we blacks are free. So join the liberation struggle. Throw off your lethargy, and the apathy of affluence. Work for a better South Africa for yourselves, ourselves, and for our children. Uproot all evil and oppression and injustice of which blacks are victims and you whites are beneficiaries, so that you won't reap the whirlwind. Join the winning side. Oppression, injustice, exploitation—all these have lost, for God is on 'our side'—on the side of justice, of peace, of reconciliation, of laughter and joy, of sharing and compassion and goodness and righteousness.

St Paul asks, 'If God be for us, who can be against us?'

8. To the White South African Community

The following two appeals, to South African whites and the media, are taken from an address entitled 'Change or Illusion', delivered at a Black Sash Conference, on 10 March 1980.

Percy Qoboza is the former editor of The World, *South Africa's leading black newspaper, which was banned by the government. Dr Motlana is a Soweto civic leader, a member of the 'Committee of Ten'.*

TO THE white community in general I say—express your commitment to change, by agreeing to accept a redistribution of wealth, and a more equitable sharing of the resources of our land. Be willing to accept voluntarily a declension in your very high standard of living. Isn't it better to lose something voluntarily, and to assist in bringing about change—political powersharing—in an orderly fashion, rather than seeing this come about through bloodshed and chaos, when you will stand to lose everything? Change your attitudes. Realise that blacks are human beings, and all we want is to be treated as such. Everything you want for yourselves is exactly what we want for ourselves and for our children—a stable family life where husband lives with wife and children, adequate housing, and proper free and compulsory education for our children.

All the current black political leaders, who are acknowledged as such by the black community, are ready to talk. It is no good engaging in a charade with leaders whom most blacks repudiate. Look at what happened to Bishop Muzorewa. Our real leaders are eminently reasonable, and I include those on Robben Island and in exile. Percy Qoboza pointed out that these were the last generation that will be ready to negotiate. Please let us talk while we can, whilst there is a real possibility of an orderly evolution to a shared society. I have dedicated myself to help bring this about, yet when you hear references to people such as Dr Motlana or Percy Qoboza or myself, you could be forgiven for thinking that we were firespouting radical Marxists who were touting Russian-made guns.

9. To the South African Broadcasting Corporation

I HAVE not given up hope for the SABC, as a heaven-sent opportunity to help change attitudes in South Africa, and to help pave the way for change. If the SABC stopped being a propaganda machine, it could begin to educate whites for change. Its interviewers would not be such supine obsequious people, bowing and scraping when they are talking to someone in authority, and being abrasive to the point of rudeness with critics of the horrendous system. I hear that the SABC went to town about the remarks of a certain magistrate, and of Bishop Mokoena regarding my character. They did not think to hear my side, because, as Percy Qoboza has said, the SABC are past masters at character assassination, and are hard put to it to recognise truth—even when it stares them in the face. I urge the SABC to have a passion for truth, and leave propaganda to the party political machines.

People are sacked for showing what Baragwanatha hospital is really like, or even Soweto. 'What is unseen does not exist, and to ignore something long enough means it will disappear'—that seems to be the motto of the SABC. You must change, and so help South Africa prepare for change.

10. The South African Council of Churches—Our Work at the Grassroots

The remainder of this Part is a look at some aspects of the SACC's work: its work for human rights, the way that the Nationalist government reacted to the SACC's political involvement, and the way that Bishop Tutu defended the Council. Clearly relations between the SACC and the government were at an all-time low in October 1979.

WE IN the SACC believe in a non-racial South Africa, where people count because they are made in the image of God. So the SACC is neither a black nor a white organisation. It is a Christian organisation with a definite bias in favour of the oppressed and the exploited ones of our society. In a small way we in the SACC offices are the first fruits of this new South Africa. We have nearly all the races of South Africa, belonging to most of the major denominations, working together as a team, headed by a General Secretary who happens to be black. The sun, so far as I can make out, still rises in the East and sets in the West, and I have not noticed that the sky has fallen because whites might have to take instructions from blacks. They are not blacks or whites. No, they are Wolfram, Thom, Anne, Margaret, Father Tutu.

The gospel of Jesus Christ teaches us that true power lies not with the powerful, but with the powerless for whom he specially cared. We are challenged by our Lord's example to work for those in prison, the poor and oppressed, the homeless and despised. The Dependents Conference (DC) is a division of the SACC—it serves banned persons, detainees, political prisoners and their families. It is responsible for the welfare of all such people when, by reason of having been imprisoned or banned, they are deprived of adequate means of support. Dependants Conference is currently looking after about 700 families of political prisoners, and has a budget of about R.700,000 per annum (1979 figures). DC arranges for relatives to visit their folk on Robben Island. You can imagine what a visit from a wife, or other relative, must mean to someone sentenced to a minimum of five years—or even life imprisonment. Through the generosity of the diocese of Capetown, DC has been able to rent a hostel to accommodate these visitors, who come from all over the country and Namibia. They can usually fit in two visits during their stay—two visits for the whole year.

Jesus said, when I was in prison you visited me—that is our mandate for this work. DC also tries to enable released political prisoners to get back to a normal life, by providing means of self-support or finding employment. We helped a man who had seven children. He died and we continued to help his family. Then the widow died, and DC is now the only source of sustenance for the seven orphaned children. Strangely enough, it is for work such as this—when we try to obey our Lord—that the SACC is in bad odour.

The Asingeni Fund came into existence in June 1976 to provide relief, and help with funeral expenses for families affected by the uprisings of that year. Most of the funds have been used to provide legal aid. We do not necessarily support the accused, or condone their alleged crimes, but believe firmly in the principle that each person is entitled to the best legal defence possible. We are assisting in the proper administration of justice, and deserve to be commended rather than to be vilified. We have had some significant statistics. In the cases where we have provided legal assistance we have notched up an acquittal rate of between 70% to 75%. Where people have been undefended, the conviction rate has been as high as 80%. Recently, through legal services that the

SACC provided, a man sentenced to twelve years on Robben Island was acquitted on appeal. One such case is justification enough for continuing this work.

Is it being emotional or melodramatic to say that it is becoming increasingly criminal to be a Christian in South Africa? Well, try employing a so-called illegal black (someone who does not possess a pass or permit to work in urban areas). You are told that it is better to increase the unemployment figures—to consign people to the scrap heap of discarded people in the resettlement camps. What is the Church of God doing about it? What are we doing about it all? I believe we should tell people who are banned to ignore their banning orders, and let us support them when there are consequences. I think the Churches should mount a massive campaign of support, through positive non-co-operation with the implementation of immoral, unchristian and unjust laws. Perhaps I should say that Churches should first urge the government to lift all banning orders forthwith, and failing this to mount a campaign.

The SACC is not always merely negative and critical of the authorities. We often send congratulatory messages to the government—we have commended Mr Botha for his courage, and praised Dr Koornhof for his reprieve of Crossroads and Alexander Township.

However, the SACC could not by any stretch of the imagination be called the blue-eyed boy of the Nationalist government. Since 1978 we have been regularly attacked by Cabinet Ministers and lesser mortals. Mr Kruger, then Minister of Justice and Police did his bit in 1978. Mr Schlebusch, his successor, warned the SACC after its National Conference of 1979 spoke in favour of supporting those who felt called to disobey state laws at variance with the law of God. Later in 1979 Mr le Grange, the new Minister for Prisons and Police, attacked the SACC quite viciously. The climax came in May 1980, when the Prime Minister himself accused the SACC of fomenting unrest in the country, using the funds it had received mainly from overseas. In September of 1979 I was called to a meeting with Mr Schlebusch and Dr Koornhof, where I was asked to retract my 'coal statement', made in Copenhagen, and apologise for having made it. I refused to do either. My passport was confiscated in February 1980, almost certainly as a punishment for my Denmark episode.

Church leaders have usually come to our support, repudiating the slurs cast against us, but it has often seemed as if we were operating in a country behind the Iron Curtain. Apart from this attention from the government, we have come under fire from the sanctimonious 'Christian League of South Africa', an organisation exposed as a front for the discredited Information Department, and one that was still receiving government funding until the end of 1979. But every time an attack has been levelled by the government or others at the SACC we have replied in strong terms against the accusations.

11. In Defence of the SACC

What follows is the text of a press statement, released on 11 October 1979, after Mr Le Grange made his attack on the SACC.

MR LOUIS LE GRANGE is quoted in newspaper reports as having made serious allegations against the SACC. My response is based on these reports which we hope are an accurate reflection of what the Minister said.

If these reports are correct then I can only say that I am deeply shocked, shocked that someone holding such a responsible position could speak so irresponsibly, so tendentiously and so untruthfully. It is distressing to find him picking up where his predecessor left off—making statements which cunningly link up the SACC and the Churches with, for instance, the Communist Party, so that there will be guilt by association and innuendo.

I want to declare categorically that I believe apartheid to be evil and immoral, and therefore unchristian. No theologian I know of would be prepared to say that the apartheid system is consistent with the Gospel of Jesus Christ. If Mr le Grange thinks that blacks are *not* exploited, repressed and denied their human rights and dignity, then I invite him to be black for just one day. He would then hear Mr Arrie Paulus saying he is like a baboon, and a senior police officer saying he is violent by nature. He would be aware that in the land of their birth, black people, who form 80% of the population, have 13% of the land, and the white minority of about 20% has 87% of the land. In this country a white child of eighteen years can vote, but a black person, be he a university professor or a bishop or whatever has no franchise. A black doctor with the same qualifications as his white counterpart is paid less for the same job. Have any whites had their homes demolished, and then been told to move to an inhospitable area, where they must live in tents until they have built themselves new houses? This happened last week to the Batlokwa people. I doubt very much that the Minister would still be able to say that apartheid was not an unchristian and unjust system, where human rights are denied.

I am sorry he speaks of propaganda actions on the part of the Churches. Fortunately, the Churches have *not* been guilty of using R.64 million to sell an unsellable commodity. (*See note for 'Message to Journalists' in Part Three.*)

Our Conference resolution on obeying God rather than man was taken by a responsible Conference, made up not of fire eating so-called leftists, but of Church leaders and duly elected representatives. The SACC and the Churches reserve the right to condemn, if need be, any legislation which is abhorrent to the Christian conscience, and which represents an abrogation of the rule of law. Certainly detention without trial, and the arbitrary banning of people are in this category, and we do not apologise for being ever vigilant in this regard.

Is the Minister aware of what he is saying when he accuses the SACC and the Churches of the crimes of providing relief for political detainees, and for providing legal defence for those involved in political trials? If these are crimes then we openly and proudly plead guilty. We declare that everybody is entitled to the best defence possible. We should be praised rather than vilified for our part in ensuring that there is an equitable administration of justice.

The SACC has been critical of the role of foreign investment, but has nowhere yet advocated, cautiously or otherwise, an anti-investment policy.

It seems it is reprehensible to condemn an educational system which is grossly lop-sided, and to advocate a more equitable distribution of resources for the greater good of an undivided South Africa. We are accused of doing something quite evil in trying to alleviate the distress of unemployed people, by helping them produce income through self-help projects. The Minister says we are exploiting the unemployment situation. We want to say, as respectfully as possible, that the Minister is talking arrant nonsense, and we would hope he would apologise for all these groundless attacks, especially this one. The Minister is guilty of gross untruths (and he knows it) when he says we have channelled funds to resistance movements. Why does he not use the wide powers he has to prosecute us, if we have done what is obviously so illegal in South Africa?

We know the tactics of this government. They plan to take action against the SACC, and they wish to prepare the public for that action. We want to remind them of a few things. First of all, they must stop playing at being God. They are human beings who happen to be carrying out an unjust and oppressive policy with a whole range of draconian laws. But they are still just mere mortals. And we are tired of having threats levelled against us. Why don't they carry them out?

Secondly, we want to warn Mr le Grange, and others who may be tempted to emulate him. The SACC is a Council of Churches, not a private organisation. The Church has been in existence for nearly 2000 years. Tyrants and others have acted against Christians during those years. They have arrested them, they have killed them, they have proscribed the faith. Those tyrants belong now to the flotsam and jetsam of forgotten history—and the

51

Church of God remains, an agent of justice, of peace, of love and reconciliation. If they take the SACC and the Churches on, let them just know they are taking on the Church of Jesus Christ.

12. Where I Stand

'Given a background such as this', wrote Bishop Tutu in Kairos, 'it was quite incredible that a meeting should take place between Church leaders and the Prime Minister.' The meeting was fixed for 7 August 1980, and three days before it took place, Bishop Tutu stated his position, in the following address given at the Pretoria Press Club.

RECENTLY, WHEN I was on a flight from Durban, one of the pretty airhostesses approached me to say: 'Excuse me, Sir, a group of passengers would like you please to autograph a book for them.' Well, I thought, there are some nice people about who show they have a good sense of values. They appreciate a good thing when they see it. I was trying to look suitably modest, when she went on to say, 'You *are* Bishop Muzorewa, aren't you?'

That was an interesting episode, which in some ways was a comment on our South African situation. Bishop Muzorewa was a great favourite of most of white South Africa. Nobody seems to have thought to use the usual bit about his bringing politics into religion. This would indicate that as long as the politics one brings in is in favour, then one is not guilty of being a political cleric. I suppose that if I was to get up and say what it is quite impossible for me to do: 'Apartheid is not too bad; it is a genuine attempt to find a solution to our intractable problems'—I would become the blue-eyed boy of the Establishment, and not a whisper would be heard of my being a political hothead. SABCTV, which last interviewed me in 1978, would probably fall over themselves to get me on the box, instead of parading people who are generally unacceptable to the black community, to refute this or that statement that I have made.

For many whites, I am regarded as an irresponsible, radical fire-eater, who should have been locked up long ago, banned or had something equally horrible happen to me. I receive some quite hair-raising letters and telephone calls. My main sadness is when my family become the target of these obscene and demented calls. Then I really get angry. I am thankful that my family support me fully, in what I believe to be God's calling to me at this time, and that as a family we know that there is some cost in being involved, as most blacks and some whites are, in the liberation struggle to make South Africa truly free for all her children, black and white. But even so, it is painful to see ones child trembling with rage and shock because she has answered one of these calls.

I don't say this to evoke sympathy, or to pretend that we are heroes. It is merely to describe one facet of the reality that is contemporary South Africa. I was quite taken aback by the hostility against me, after my remark in Denmark about purchases of South African coal. It was as if I had said: 'Blacks go on the rampage and rape every white woman in sight.' I don't think I could have aroused greater animosity if I had in fact been guilty of that sort of incitement to racial hatred and violence. In fact what I said was an attempt to make a sober contribution to finding a solution to our South African problem, without using violence. People are quite happy to talk about so-called peaceful means of change, as long as you canvass methods that everybody knows will be ineffectual; for basically, most whites want change as long as things remain the same, as long as they can go on enjoying their privileges and their high standard of living. That is why we urge the international community to exert as much political, diplomatic and economic pressure on South Africa as possible, to persuade us to get to the conference table. I love South Africa too passionately to want to see her destroyed, and international pressure may just avert that. And so in the perception of most whites in South Africa I am an ogre—something they will use to frighten children into obedience. I am, so they say, really a politician trying hard to be a bishop, and I manage with consummate skill to hide my horns under my funny bishop's hat, and my tail tucked away under my trailing cope.

But in reality I have no political ambitions whatsoever. In this respect I am no Bishop Muzorewa, Archbishop Makarios or Ayatollah Khomeini. (Indeed these gentlemen could be said to provide three reasons why religious leaders should not be politicians in the party political sense.) As I have said, it is my Christian faith which constrains me to behave in the way that I do. For me, through my fallible understanding of the scriptures, apartheid can only be described as blasphemous, and therefore I cannot but oppose it with every fibre in my being, and try to do all that I can, nationally and internationally, to have it changed.

Some say I want to promote a confrontation with the state. Nothing could be further from the truth. I believe fervently that when the state does the things that are proper to it, then it commands obedience. But when it exceeds its bounds, when it wants to claim what belongs to God for itself, then it is a religious duty to condemn this abuse of power, for Jesus said 'Render unto Caesar the things that are Caesar's, and to God the things that are God's.' When the laws have been passed by the people, or through their democratically elected representatives, and when the laws are just, then they must be obeyed. But South Africa's laws fail to pass that stringent test. None of them have been passed by the people's democratically elected representatives, because 80% of the people are excluded from the democratic process of law-making, and many of the laws, the whole apartheid system, is patently unjust.

So apartheid is a system which is not only unjust, but totally immoral and totally unchristian. Its claim that God created us human beings for separation, for apartness, and for division, contradicts the Bible and the whole tradition of undivided Christendom. God has created us for fellowship, for community, for friendship with God, and with one another, so that we can live in harmony with the rest of creation as well. For my part, the day will never come when apartheid will be acceptable. It is an evil system and it is at variance with the gospel of Jesus Christ. That is why I oppose it and can never compromise with it—not for political reasons but because I am a Christian.

13. Bishop Tutu's Testimony

The meeting between the SACC and the government, came about after requests from the SACC for a meeting to discuss the continuing critical situation in South Africa. Any hopes that there would be positive results were soon to be dashed. In fact, following this meeting relations between the government and the SACC became even more confrontational.

In addition the government managed to make political capital out of it, while the SACC lost some credibility amongst some black Christians. But while one might be justified as regarding it as an occasion when the SACC was out maneouvred by the government, this meeting stands out as a courageous act on the SACC's part, an attempt at reconciliation and bridge building.

Bishop Tutu's own attitude towards the meeting is that 'it was not a conversation—there was a very wide gulf between the two sides. But it was a good thing that we tried to sit side by side, instead of fighting each other.'

What follows is Bishop Tutu's statement to the government.

WE HAVE no political axes to grind, and I think that should be stressed. The same gospel of Jesus Christ, which compels us to reject apartheid as totally unchristian, is the very gospel that constrains us to work for justice, for peace and reconciliation. God has given us a mandate to be ministers of His reconciliation.

We thank God that you and your government have come to recognise that the destiny of the peoples of South Africa cannot be decided by one group alone. We want to urge you, yet again, to negotiate for orderly change, by calling a National Convention, where our common future can be mapped out by the acknowledged leaders of every section of the South African population. To this end we believe fervently that the political prisoners in jail, in detention, in exile, must be permitted to attend such a convention. After all, your predecessor Mr Vorster counselled Mr Ian Smith to release black political prisoners, and sit around a conference table with them to try and hammer out a solution for their country.

It was your government which tried out a scheme similar to this in the Turnhalle talks relating to Namibia. Why should this way of dealing with apparently intractable problems be one that is for export only?

We believe that there can be no real peace in our beloved land until there is fundamental change. General Malan has said that the crisis in South Africa is 20% military and 80% political. You yourself have courageously declared that whites must be ready to adapt or die. This adapting, or change, has to go to the heart of the matter—to the dismantling of apartheid. Please believe us when we say there is much goodwill left, although we have to add that time and patience are running out. Hatred, bitterness and anger are growing, and unless something is done to demonstrate your intentions to bring about fundamental change, leading to power sharing, then we are afraid that the so-called ghastly alternative will be upon us. We recognise that this kind of fundamental change cannot happen overnight, and so we suggest that only four things need be done to give real hope that this change is going to happen. We can assure you that if we go along this road, you will gain most of South Africa and the world, while losing some of your party dissidents. These are the four points:

(1) LET THE GOVERNMENT COMMIT THEMSLVES TO A COMMON CITIZENSHIP IN AN UNDIVIDED SOUTH AFRICA.

If this does not happen we will have to kiss goodbye to peaceful change.

(2) PLEASE ABOLISH THE PASS LAWS.

Nothing is more hateful in a hateful system for blacks than these laws. Let it be a phased process, because none of us want to have a chaotic country. But I wish God could give me the words that could describe the dramatic change that would occur in relationships in this country, if the real abolition of the Pass Laws were to happen.

(3) PLEASE STOP IMMEDIATELY ALL POPULATION REMOVALS AND THE UPROOTING OF PEOPLE.

It is in my view totally evil and has caused untold misery.

(4) SET UP A UNIFORM EDUCATIONAL SYSTEM.

We are glad to note that you have agreed to the calling up of a commission to look into this matter. We want to suggest, in relation to this, that all universities be declared open, and that the black universities be free to appoint blacks who have credibility in the black community. Otherwise we fear that the unrest in these institutions will remain endemic.

If these four things were done, as starters, then we would be the first to declare out loud: please give the government a chance, they seem in our view to have embarked on the course of real change. I certainly would be one of the first to shout this out from the rooftops. For then, through that process, we would all have *real* security, not a security that depends on force for its upholding. What a wonderful country we can have when we all, black and white, walk out heads high to this glorious future together. Because we will have a non-racial society, a just society, where everyone, black and white, is a child of God, created in his image. And you sir, will go down in history as a truly great man.

If this does not happen now, urgently, then I fear we will have to say we have had it. But God is good, and God loves all of us, and God has filled this country with his Holy Spirit. Let us be open to that Holy Spirit and share our fears and anxieties. Thank you.

In the Prime Minister's closing address it became clear that the SACC had not managed to convince the government of the need for real change—political powersharing—in South Africa. 'I am prepared to lead my people on the road . . . to create new dispensations,' he said, 'but I am not prepared to lead them on the road of a government of one man one vote.'

Part Three
Windows into South Africa

14. Steve Biko—A Tribute

The singularly brutal way in which Steve Biko met his death at the hands of the South African Security Police outraged and saddened people throughout the world. Detained in Port Elizabeth on 18 August 1977, under Section 6 of the Terrorism Act, he was taken in chains to Pretoria—a bumping, bruising journey of 600 miles—in the back of a police landrover. He died, aged thirty-one, after being kept naked and manacled, in detention on 12 September, as a result of the beatings he received in custody.

Steve Biko, thinker and activist, was born in Kingwilliamstown on 18 December 1946. In the late 1960s he formed SASO, the South African Students Organisation, and organised and wrote— sometimes under the name Frank Talk—until he was banned in March 1973. He was especially concerned with the building up of pride and awareness amongst his people, by demonstrating the worth of African culture, and by careful analysis of the processes by which the white settlers had stripped the black population of their freedom. This was the Black Consciousness Movement, which found expression in the rapidly outlawed Black People's Convention. He is now regarded as the founder of this movement. He called on black ministers of religion to support the cause of Black Consciousness by restoring direction and meaning to the black man's understanding of God.

The following tribute is taken from Bishop Tutu's oration at his funeral in Kingwilliamstown, and from his address at the SACC Memorial Service for Steve Biko, held at St George's Cathedral, Capetown.

WHEN WE heard the news 'Steve Biko is dead' we were struck numb with disbelief. No, it can't be true! No, it must be a horrible nightmare, and we will awake and find that really it is different— that Steve is alive even if it be in detention. But no, dear friends, he is dead and we are still numb with grief, and groan with anguish

'Oh God, where are you? Oh God, do you really care—how can you let this happen to us?'

It all seems such a senseless waste of a wonderfully gifted person, struck down in the bloom of youth, a youthful bloom that some wanted to see blighted. What can be the purpose of such wanton destruction? God, do you really love us? What must we do which we have not done, what must we say which we have not said a thousand times over, oh, for so many years—that all we want is what belongs to all God's children, what belongs as an inalienable right—a place in the sun in our own beloved mother country. Oh God, how long can we go on? How long can we go on appealing for a more just ordering of society where we all, black and white together, count not because of some accident of birth or a biological irrelevance—where all of us black and white count because we are human persons, human persons created in your own image.

God called Steve Biko to be his servant in South Africa—to speak up on behalf of God, declaring what the will of this God must be in a situation such as ours, a situation of evil, injustice, oppression and exploitation. God called him to be the founder father of the Black Consciousness Movement against which we have had tirades and fulminations. It is a movement by which God, through Steve, sought to awaken in the Black person a sense of his intrinsic value and worth as a child of God, not needing to apologise for his existential condition as a black person, calling on blacks to glorify and praise God that he had created them black. Steve, with his brilliant mind that always saw to the heart of things, realised that until blacks asserted their humanity and their personhood, there was not the remotest chance for reconciliation in South Africa. For true reconciliation is a deeply personal matter. It can happen only between persons who assert their own personhood, and who acknowledge and respect that of others. You don't get reconciled to your dog, do you? Steve knew and believed fervently that being pro-black was not the same thing as being anti-white. The Black Consciousness Movement is not a 'hate white movement', despite all you may have heard to the contrary. He had a far too profound respect for persons as persons, to want to deal with them under readymade, shopsoiled categories.

All who met him had this tremendous sense of a warm-hearted man, and as a notable acquaintance of his told me, a man who was utterly indestructible, of massive intellect and yet reticent; quite unshakeable in his commitment to principle and to radical change in South Africa by peaceful means; a man of real reconciliation, truly an instrument of God's peace, unshakeable in his commitment to the liberation of all South Africans, black and white, striving for a more just and more open South Africa.

Steve saw, more than most of us, how injustice and oppression can dehumanise and make us all, black and white, victim and perpetrator alike, less than what God intended us to be. Now it has always sounded like sloganeering when people have said 'Oppression dehumanises the oppressor as well as the oppressed.' But have we not had an unbelievably shocking example of this, if he has been quoted correctly, in Mr Kruger's heartless remark that Steve's death 'leaves him cold'? Of all human beings, he is the most to be pitied. What has happened to him as a human being when the death of a fellow human being can leave him cold? And I bid you pray for the rulers of this land, for the police—especially the security police and those in the prison service—that they may realise that they are human beings too. I bid you pray for whites in South Africa.

It is no cheap slogan to say that Black Consciousness seeks, as Steve saw, the liberation of both black and white. Black Consciousness, in being concerned for black liberation, was, and is utterly committed, equally, to white liberation.

It was a man who was saying these things, it was a man who inspired us to share these thoughts, it was a man who infused others to a like commitment to justice, love, peace, reconciliation—all in South Africa—it was such a man that death, a mysterious death, struck down last Monday. We mourn such a tragic and apparently meaningless wasteful loss, the death of a splendid leader, already at the height of his powers, while still so young.

Let us pray for Ntsiki and all of Steve's family in this death. We weep for our land which has suffered a grievous blow, we weep for ourselves and yet we know that Steve lived his life as one that was always being laid down for his friends and his enemies; so that his death, ghastly as it is, was a consummation of such a life—the greatest love a person can have for his friends is to lay down his life for them. Steve knew other words which that other remarkable young man, Jesus, had uttered. 'In truth, in very truth, I tell you, a grain of wheat remains a solitary grain unless it falls into the ground and dies; but if it dies, it bears a rich harvest. The man who loves himself is lost, but he who hates himself in this world will be kept safe for eternal life. If anyone serves me, he must follow me; where I am, my servant will be. Whoever serves me will be honoured by my Father.' (John 12. 24–26)

So you see, Steve has started something that is quite unstoppable. The powers of evil, of injustice, of oppression, of exploitation, have done their worst and they have lost. They have lost because they are immoral and wrong, and our God, the God of Exodus, the liberator God, is a God of justice and righteousness, and he is on the side of justice and liberation and goodness. Our cause, the cause of justice and liberation, must triumph because it is moral and just and right. Many who support the present unjust system in this country, know in their hearts that they are upholding a system that is evil and unjust and oppressive, and which is utterly abhorrent and displeasing to God. There is no doubt whatsoever that freedom is coming. (Yes, it may be a costly struggle still, but we are experiencing today the birth pangs of a new South Africa.) The darkest hour, they say, is before the dawn. We are experiencing the birth pangs of a new South Africa, a free South Africa, where all of us, black and white together, will walk tall, where all of us, black and white together, will hold hands as we stride forth on the Freedom March, to usher in the new South Africa. We thank and praise God for giving us such a magnificent gift in Steve Biko, and for his sake, and the sake of ourselves and our children, let us dedicate ourselves anew to the struggle for the liberation of our beloved land, South Africa.

1. Nelson Mandela. His speech from the dock in the Rivonia Trial is one of the classic statements of African Nationalism. He has been imprisoned on Robben Island since 1964. (*Photo: Eli Weinberg*)

2. Robert Sobukwe. 'When the annals of this our beloved country are rewritten the name of Robert Mangaliso Sobukwe will be etched in letters of gold.'

3. Steve Biko. 'He had far too profound a respect for persons as persons to want to deal with them under ready made, shop-soiled categories.'

Steve Biko's son Samora, his wife Ntsiki, and mourners at his funeral at King-williamstown.

5. The procession at Steve Biko's funeral.

6. Part of Soweto. (*photo: Abisag Tullman*)

7. A white residential area. (*photo: Tony McGrath/IDAF*)

8. Demonstrators lie dead minutes after the police opened fire at Sharpeville. (*photo: Ian Berry*)

9. Troop carriers confront demonstrators in an incident during the Soweto riots of 1976.

10. Children and the Crossroads Squatter camp, 1978. (*photo: Steve Bloom/IDAF*)

11. Student groups who hijacked two buses on their way to the funeral of the 'Silverton Seige' three. (*photo: RDM*)

12. Mrs Winnie Mandela.

13. Nelson Mandela outside Westminster Abbey, 1962.

14. Prisoners breaking rocks in the courtyard of Robben Island maximum security prison.

15. Bishop Desmond Tutu, Mrs Leah Tutu, and the Revd Thomas Anthony, a visiting Canadian minister, leaving court after spending one night in police custody in John Vorster Square. (*photos 1–15 courtesy IDAF*)

16. Bishop Desmond Tutu in London Spring 1981. (*photo: Camera Press*)

15. Robert Mangaliso Sobukwe

Robert Sobukwe was born in 1924, in the Cape Province. He was active in the non-violent protest campaigns of the 1950s, losing his job as a teacher for taking part in the Defiance Campaign of 1952. In the late 1950s he was instrumental in setting up the Pan Africanist Congress (PAC), which broke away from the African National Congress (ANC) in 1959. He was elected its president, and resigned from his post of lecturer in African Languages at the University of Witwatersrand to lead the anti-pass law protests in 1960. These protests were greeted with an infamous display of state violence: at Sharpeville, on 21 March 1960, the police opened fire on the unarmed crowd, killing 67 people, and wounding 186.

Robert Sobukwe was arrested and sentenced to three years imprisonment, and on his release, was detained on Robben Island for six years, by a special Act of Parliament. Released in 1969, he was then banned, and confined to the district of Kimberley. Affectionately known as 'the Prof.', he died in 1978.

This tribute is the text of the address delivered by Bishop Tutu at the SACC memorial service, 6 March 1978.

LAST SEPTEMBER, I was privileged to take part in a memorial service in St Georges Cathedral, Cape Town, for Steve Biko—that grand stalwart of Africa—little thinking that only a matter of six months later I would be participating in a memorial service for an even grander stalwart, a giant among men, Robert Mangaliso Sobukwe. As it happened on the day of the memorial for Steve Biko I went to Groote Schuur Hospital to see the Prof. He had just had a major operation to remove a large section of his diseased lung. And there he was sitting in a comfortable chair, with that quite inimitable smile, speaking rather hoarsely and making little of his anguish. You know, we have often prostituted the English language so that we find we have to use quite outlandish superlatives to make our points, because ordinary straightforward

65

words are now so hackneyed that they have lost their original significance. Hence Hollywood will tell us of a stupendous extravaganza and what have you. Despite this devaluation of language, I want to speak soberly without superlatives.

When you met Robert you knew without a shadow of doubt that you had met a great man. He had an outstanding intellect and yet walked with the humblest who felt at home in his company. He was too great to have a base or mean thought, and so quite amazingly he was untouched by bitterness, despite the unjust and cruel experiences he underwent for what he believed with all the fibre of his being. Even his most determined opponents had to admit that his was an attractive and magnetic personality. All who met him fell under the spell of his irresistible smile and charm. Even the Security Police ate out of his hand. They could not help it. He had the gentleness of a dove and yet he had the unshaken firmness of the person of principle. The years on Robben Island failed to change his beliefs.

I don't use these words lightly or glibly. He was a holy man, devoted to Jesus Christ his Lord and Master, and for that reason committed to seeing radical change happening in South Africa without violence and bloodshed, death and destruction. The tragedy of this country is that the powers that be have consistently refused to parley with such as Robert. And they may still live to regret missing such a grand opportunity, because they can't say of Robert what they said of Steve—that he was a virtual unknown— for Robert was a considerable political force to reckon with. And all South Africa could do with one of the greatest of her sons was to muzzle him, to banish and attempt to emasculate. What tragic and unmitigated waste. But when the annals of this our beloved country are rewritten, the name of Robert Mangaliso Sobukwe will be etched in letters of gold—for despite what they tried to do to him his spirit and his ideas broke through these fetters, and transcended the human restraints, and his spirit and his thoughts have lived on in the Black Consciousness Movement. I am sad that the University of the Witwatersrand, which was privileged because he taught there, never thought to honour one of the brightest stars in its firmament, and I hope that institution may still rectify this ghastly omission by a posthumous award.

And what about us? Must we mourn—Yes, to some extent for the going hence of a human being diminishes each of us. But let us not mourn disconsolately and long, because Robert would not have it so. We have offered in sacrifice some of the best of our people, and our struggle for justice, and for the ending of oppression and exploitation, is a moral struggle, and God is on our side. Robert knew he was part of a winning side. Victory is assured. Freedom is coming to South Africa for all of us. About that there is no doubt. God has assured us of this—our God, the liberator God of the Exodus. The questions still to be answered are how and when freedom will come. Robert worked and prayed that it would come soon and come peacefully. And we are with him in this struggle and prayer.

16. Polarisation

The Tate-Coetzee fight was the first occasion that a South African (white) fought for the World Heavyweight boxing title.

I AM really distressed at the degree of polarisation that exists in our country. Last year I was working away until about midnight one Saturday night when the quiet of Soweto was shattered by car hooters blaring, and general pandemonium of the sort we associate with New Year's Eve in the townships. Then I remembered—it was the big Tate-Coetzee fight. 'I'm sure Tate has won,' I said to myself. I switched on the radio (I hardly ever listen to the SABC. We vowed in our house that we would not get a TV set until the SABC provides us with a propaganda free service.) And my guess was confirmed. Most blacks in South Africa were thrilled that Tate had won (even those who were totally opposed to Tate's coming to fight in South Africa in the first place). They were thrilled because Tate was black, but also because he had made a South African white bite the dust. Most whites were despondent as a result of that defeat. It was as if it was a defeat on the battlefield. It certainly was more than just a sporting event for both sides. Somehow it was seen on one side as a blow against the so-called traditional South African way of life, and on the other as a slightly traumatic happening—something not too good for the South African white psyche.

I could go on to give a whole sorry catalogue of issues on which we are sadly divided on racial lines. On the matter of foreign investments most whites are in favour of increased investments, whereas I suspect (you can't speak about this openly) most blacks would wish to use this as a means for exerting pressure for real and meaningful change. Most whites were delighted when the British Lions came; not so blacks. Most whites were overjoyed that Margaret Thatcher's Conservative Party came to power, and you can be sure that most blacks were saddened by this election result. Actually you could become a kind of Euclid and propound an axiom: whatever pleases most white South Africans is almost certain to displease most blacks and vice versa.

17. Banned People

Banning orders are frequently used to silence opponents of apartheid. Those who are banned may be subjected to house arrest, cannot associate or communicate with more than one person, and their articles, recordings or books cannot be quoted or distributed in South Africa. Just how petty and inhuman the banning orders are is well illustrated by the following story, told by Bishop Tutu in a sermon preached in Kingston, Jamaica, on the feast of Epiphany, 1979.

I VISITED one of these banned people, Winnie Mandela. Her husband, Nelson Mandela, is serving a life sentence on Robben Island, our maximum security prison. I wanted to take her Holy Communion. The police told me I couldn't enter her house. So we celebrated Holy Communion in my car in the street in Christian South Africa. On a second occasion I went to see her on a weekend. Her restriction order is more strict at weekends. She can't leave her yard. So we celebrated Holy Communion again in the street. This time Winnie was on one side of the fence and I on the other. This in Christian South Africa in 1978.

18. Detention without Trial

Under the Terrorism Act of 1967, the police in South Africa have the power to detain opponents of apartheid indefinitely, without any access to families, solicitors or courts. And as if that was not enough, people often emerge from detention to find they have had a banning order served on them. This is a press statement, dated 20 November 1978.

WE REJOICE in the release of several people at the weekend from lengthy periods of detention. But why in God's name should they then be banned for five years without the opportunity of stating their side of the case?

The police have had more than enough time—394 days—to build cases against these people. Our deepest distress is that so very few white South Africans seem to care about this abrogation of the rule of law. We appeal yet again to the authorities of this land to move our society away from the brink of disaster. If whites do not care, God cares.

19. Urban Unrest

Press Statement, 17 June 1980.

WE DEPLORE all the violence that erupted over the weekend and we regret especially the death of one policeman. But we want to emphasise firmly that to tell people when they can mourn, and when they can't, is really to ask for trouble. The black community has been very deeply hurt by this insensitive ban on what have always been in the past peaceful, dignified, and solemn occasions. Afrikaners would be angered if one day they were told they cannot commemorate the day of the Covenant.

Please for God's sake let us stop playing with fire. I want to warn the authorities that their efforts at maintaining law and order will succeed only in producing a sullen and bitter lull. The situation in our country is highly volatile, and only meaningful discussions between the Prime Minister and at least Church leaders, with the intention of bringing about real change in South Africa, can deal with a rapidly deteriorating situation. We appeal with all our eloquence at our command for such a meeting. The black community can be dealt with effectively only through its own recognised leaders. Anything else the Government attempts will be like fiddling while the fires of revolution burn in our country.

We place ourselves unreservedly at the disposal of the authorities to work with them for justice, peace, law and order and reconciliation. Please will somebody hear us, please hear us before it is too late.

20. Armed soldiers on routine police matters

Press Statement, 3 April 1978.

LAST FRIDAY 31 March, the police carried out a combined operation with the army and traffic police in what one newspaper described as a blitz. The police have to do their duty to maintain law and order, and to apprehend all lawbreakers and criminals. But I wish to express considerable disquiet that in carrying out their normal duties the police should have been assisted by army personnel armed with rifles and fixed bayonets. A senior police officer is reported to have described this combined operation as 'routine'. Nowhere in the free world is such a practice regarded as routine, when there is no civil disturbance or breakdown of law and order.

In the name of God and good sense, I want to appeal to the authorities to desist from the practice of employing armed soldiers on routine police matters. What happened on Friday can only be described as a very provocative action—many of those who were stopped were very tired, ordinary, decent law abiding people, intent on getting home quickly out of the rain.

I want to protest very strongly about the body searches carried out on women by those manning the road blocks. One of my senior staff was subjected to this humiliating indignity. The police and authorities require the co-operation and assistance of the public in their difficult work of preventing crime, but last Friday's action was not calculated to win them any friends in the black community.

21. A better approach

Ever since the Soweto riots of June 1976, the anniversaries of 16 June have been occasions fraught with tension. The behaviour of the police on these occasions is often a contributory factor in the outbreak of violence, and here Bishop Tutu praises them for sensible conduct on one of these anniversaries.

ON BEHALF of the South African Council of Churches, I wish to commend the police very warmly for keeping a very low profile during the services commemorating 16 June.

As many responsible blacks have pointed out in the past, there were hardly any incidents to mar what were mainly peaceful and dignified observances. We hope this is a style the police will adopt more and more to the benefit of our country.

22. The Pass Laws

The Pass Laws are designed to keep the black population 'in their place', by controlling their movement; restricting them to the 'homelands', or to the Townships where they have the status of migrant labourers, or to short stays in adjoining 'white' urban areas. The Pass Laws are the mechanism by which white South Africa keeps the wealth and property of the country in its own hands, shutting blacks out from the industrial areas where employment and money are concentrated. The Pass Laws deliberately destroy family life, usually denying the migrant worker the right to have his family with him, and exemplify the convoluted thinking upon which apartheid is based. This is a Press Statement from 1979.

NINETEEN YEARS ago, blacks protested peacefully for the abolition of the Pass Laws, which are the most resented feature of a hated system. The passes, more than anything else in South Africa, demonstrate that the black person is a second class citizen in the land of his birth.

For a while it seemed that these Pass Laws were being administered with decreasing hardness, since pass raids were not apparently being carried out as conspicuously as formerly. But the statistics for 1978 show an increase of 100,000 in those arrested for Pass offences. Pass raids are becoming once again a feature of the South African scene. Perhaps this is an attempt by the authorities to remove unemployed blacks from the urban areas—to dump them in the bantustans, so that it will be a case of out of sight, out of mind. But arrests are also being made among people who are obviously working, or are students—most of them not being given the time to produce their passes, in violation of a Supreme Court ruling.

It appears from this that there is a deliberate stepping up of the harassment of blacks, otherwise why carry out raids even amongst people returning from work?

With all the eloquence I can command I appeal to the authorities to stop this harassment and humiliation of black people. Pass raids are highly provocative in a situation where tension is growing, due to high unemployment amongst black people. In the name of God and of Christian charity, let us beware that we are not deliberately leading up to another disastrous confrontation between the black community and the police; with consequent bloodshed, loss of life, destruction of property, and violence.

I am distressed by the apparent silence of our white fellow South Africans, over these latest developments. All of this is being done in your name. Do you acquiesce in something that has such potentially disastrous consequences? Don't say you are impotent. You can do something if you are opposed to what is happening. Beware of the legacy of hatred that the police action is building up amongst blacks. Assist for God's sake, act for your children's sake and for South Africa's sake.

23. Christmas

Press Statement, 20 November 1978.

CHRISTMAS IS a season of goodwill, of joy, but for many in our beloved land it is also a bleak time, a time of watching others enjoy good things without themselves having anything to enjoy. It is a time when deprivation is all the more starkly realised by those who have little, because of the excesses of those who have so much.

We believe it is right to herald the birthday of our Lord and liberator with joy and thanksgiving. We believe also that joy is increased when shared with others, that thanksgiving is the more real the more it is shared.

In this spirit of sharing we would appeal to those in business and industry to make available vacation jobs for those young people who will shortly go on holiday. In these days of rising unemployment it is becoming more and more difficult for parents to afford to give their children adequate educational opportunities. For some young people their only hope of being able to further their education is by making extra money to help their parents. The SACC is receiving daily requests for such temporary employment, and would be most willing to act as a clearing agency, to fit applicants to available jobs.

We appeal for this season of goodwill to be shared, in the name of Him whose coming we celebrate.

24. Crossroads

Because the 'homelands' are so impoverished, and have so few employment prospects, people move out—forced out by starvation— to try and find work elsewhere. As this is an illegal act there is no official accommodation provided for them, and consequently shanty towns are set up near Townships, both by people looking for work, and by people who want to live together as families. The incredible fact is that even if one has to spend nine months of the year in prison, for violating the Pass Laws, one can still earn more in the remaining three months than in a whole year in the 'homelands'.

The first shanties of Crossroads, the camp in the Cape Province near the townships of Nyanga and Guguletu, were set up in February 1975. The people were subjected to constant harassment, with the whole dreary scene of mass arrests, pass raids, and destruction of shacks being acted out by the police. In February 1977 eviction notices were served, and in August 1977 one of the camps in the settlement was demolished. (Surely the police had better things to do with their time?) In November 1978, Dr Koornhof, the government minister, bowed to pressure from the world community, and declared he was 'willing to regularise the position' of the Crossroads camp, and granted a stay of execution of the eviction order. Crossroads was saved, but unfortunately this did not mean that the government had decided on a change of policy towards the squatter camps in the country. In August 1981, police evicted people from the Nyanga settlement, in yet another particularly heartless operation, that yet again exposed the moral bankruptcy of the apartheid system. (Press Statement, 16 May 1978.)

I VISITED Crossroads twice last Wednesday. In the afternoon I went to see the Mobile Clinic and the school; the children sang and one of their songs told why Crossroads and places like it have happened—'Matanzima has no money'—the homelands are not financially viable. And then I met some of those extraordinary women who have decided they are going to be what they said they were going to be when they took their marriage vows—husbands' wives. One of them said to me, when I asked what she would do when they demolished Crossroads: 'Umfundisi, we will just take our belongings and go elsewhere to start another camp. If they want my husband here, working for them, then they will have to want me and my children.' That is the spirit of Crossroads—a dignified confidence that they are right in wanting to be families.

The second time I visited Crossroads was in the evening of that

Wednesday—I preached at the regular Wednesday evening service, which was started to show the solidarity of those who live in the townships, with the squatters. There were over 500 people in the Hall. I am quite sure that it is immoral and unchristian to want to destroy family life, *especially* in a country that has a public holiday called—'Family Day'. So I add my voice to those who plead with the authorities to change their minds, even at this late stage. Do not destroy Crossroads. You are destroying a community and South Africa cannot afford that.

25. R.14,000,000 and all that

A piece in reply to a journalist, who asked Bishop Tutu what he would do with a sudden windfall. It is dated 17 November 1978.

OF COURSE, you must pinch me to ensure that I am not really dreaming. Imagine R.14,000,000 to spend as I wish! Others, as we have come to learn, have had considerable practice in how to lighten their heavy load of shekels. I can assure you that I am just a rank amateur in this game and I will perform like a raw recruit. Because of my lack of experience I have decided that I want to put forward my basic ideas and let an expert work out the details. After all, that is what we do when we want to build a house. We go to the architect and let him have our ideas, then he translates our vision into reality.

The really crying need among our people is adequate housing. A house makes you feel you have arrived, that you belong, and that you are not a bird of passage. It gives you roots, so I would want to do my bit to ease the ghastly shortage of proper housing. And I don't mean just a matchbox structure. Our black people have shown, that given the opportunity and the right kind of assistance—which has almost always been available to whites, Indians and coloureds, that they erect splendid buildings. I would

76

want my kind of house to be one that filled its owners with a proper kind of pride.

Then I would want to invest in a scheme that would make community services available—of the kind that other sections of the South African population take for granted. I am talking about tarred streets, proper sewerage, paved sidewalks to save us from the dust that plays havoc with our health and our smartly polished shoes. I would want proper streetlighting, to make our townships less attractive to the denizens of night, who are encouraged to perform their nefarious tasks by our ill-lit streets. It goes without saying that my scheme would ensure that we had electrified townships, so that we did not have to spend so much on coal, candles and paraffin. The smog that hangs over our townships in the early morning and evenings would be a thing of the past. Imagine the improvement in our health, that we would register almost immediately.

It would be a luxury, perhaps, but I think we appreciate beautiful things too. So I would invest some of my munificence in creating parks with flowers and trees and grass, for lovers to walk around in, arm in arm, and have laughing children gambolling like frisky lambs on the shaven lawns. You could even throw in a few swimming pools, tennis courts and playgrounds to keep our children off the streets. I would want to see more libraries and places where people could learn wholesome hobbies.

I would then put most of what remained after my community 'binge' into education   into pre-school creches, into well-built and well-equipped primary schools with libraries and, wonder of wonders, well-equipped laboratories. *We learned Science by imagining the various experiments*. I would keep some of the education funds for bursaries, to enable our children to further their education, here and abroad.

I would keep some of my funds to help get people out of the claustrophobic atmosphere of South Africa— get them to meet other people in different parts of the world so that they could experience what it means to be really human. It is a liberating experience.

I would leave a little to pay the accountant to see that I did not fiddle the books.

26. Black Consciousness and Car Driving

An article of 9 November 1978, arising from the daily journey from the township of Soweto to work in Johannesburg. The government has now embarked on a scheme to bring electricity to Soweto.

LONG LINES of traffic, interminably snaking along from the different parts of Soweto early in the morning. Everybody is on their way to join the ratrace in their different places of work. Tempers get frayed, exhausts belch thick black smoke, scooters are the only things that seem to make any headway.

We repeat this saga of the procession of cars, buses, lorries and combies in the evening as we rush home—home with the haze hanging over our houses. I wish Soweto could be electrified. Our health for one thing would benefit, and just think of the saving, the cleanliness and the general improvement in our lives.

Here we are all sitting in this slow moving line of cars, trying to look unflustered, and gaining credit for developing the virtue of patience, when quite suddenly you see these cars—almost all of them taxis—flashing past this long line. They are travelling where the oncoming traffic is supposed to move. Sometimes you can see the traffic that is moving in the opposite direction flashing its headlights, to show these maverick cars the recklessness of their driving. Sometimes the cars which have the right of way are forced to swerve out of the way of these smart drivers. They obviously think that those who snake along slowly are stupid, and yet their driving is reckless, and they are endangering the lives of other road users. No wonder we have such ghastly accidents in and around our townships.

What is the remedy? A short term remedy would be to have traffic policemen patrolling these routes during the rush hours, ticketting the reckless drivers without mercy. But that is an unsatisfactory solution. Much the best solution is that we blacks show that we do have a proper pride in ourselves—that is what black consciousness is all about. We have a proper pride and self respect. And if I respect myself, then I will respect other blacks. And that respect has a great deal to do with how I drive. Why don't these smart drivers do their awful thing in town? Well, they are afraid of whites and they really despise themselves and other blacks. They need to be spiritually liberated not to despise themselves or other blacks.

That is black consciousness and car driving.

27. A Message to Journalists

The following two passages, dealing with the role of the press in society, both contain references to the 'Muldergate' affair. This political scandal involved Dr Connie Mulder, ex-Minister of Information, who was exposed as running a slush fund from which clandestine payments were made to promote South Africa's image at home and abroad. Allegations started appearing in the South African press in 1977 about the existence of this fund, which, it was suggested, had funded the pro-government 'Citizen' newspaper, as well as paying out large sums to politicians in Britain and the USA, to protect South African interests. By the end of 1978 further leaks to the press conclusively proved Dr Mulder's involvement, and in April 1979 he was forced to resign his ministerial post and later his membership of Parliament. The scandal continued with the revelation that State President Vorster had also been centrally involved, and he was forced to resign as well. The amount of money involved was R.64 million (about £30 million).

I THINK to be a journalist is a vocation, a calling filled with the joys of work well done, and the frustration of being often impeded in your search after the truth. There are those who do not want the truth to have too much scope, because truth can often be a dangerous commodity. It can make or break men and women, as we very well know from recent history in the United States and our own country, in those episodes known as Watergate and Muldergate. Yours *is* a high calling, because you are searchers after truth, and when you have found it, you are obliged to disseminate it, as far as is humanly possible, without distortion or embellishment. It can be a very costly and demanding vocation, because the powerful are not loath to use their power to crush those who have information which could have embarrassing or even disastrous consequences for them. I want to commend you as a fraternity for trying to be true to the highest ideals and traditions of your profession, as when you refuse to be intimidated into conformity, or into breaking confidences, even if to do so might land you in jail.

You are watchdogs for the nation, especially for the little men and women who can be manipulated, and treated shabbily by those who have power. You have an almost religious duty to come out on their behalf, to be like the Church of Jesus Christ; the voice of the voiceless, speaking up against the abuse of power, and standing up for the victims of oppression, exploitation and injustice. You must be the eyes of a society so often lulled into complacency, so that it can look and *see* how God's children are shunted from pillar to post, or left to starve, just because a racist ideology decrees that their community must be destroyed, because it is a black settlement on white land. You must be the ears of a society whose hearing has grown dull, so that it can hear the anguished cries of black mothers and children, left behind in an unviable, barren 'homeland', trying to eke out a miserable existence in some rural backwater, because South Africa's economy is based on the Migratory Labour System—a system that even the white Dutch Reformed Church condemned as a cancer in our society.

You have a crucial role to play in a South Africa that is in crisis.

Whether you like it or not, you are powerful people and you help form public opinion. Many people read nothing beyond their newspapers. Many people, especially in South Africa, have seldom exercised their critical faculties, and so hardly ever question what they read. You carry a heavy responsibility. Some of the things you write may not seem too important, yet they go a long way to forming attitudes and perceptions.

I recall how many years ago the English press described an accident like this: 'Three persons and one native were injured'— giving unconscious expression to and confirming whites in their belief that 'natives' were human but . . . I am sure the fact that most newspapers nowadays address everybody, black and white, as Mr or Miss or Mrs must have an effect on racial attitudes, even if that effect is imperceptible.

Nobody can doubt that you help to reinforce certain points of view when you describe particular groups either as terrorists or freedom fighters or insurgents. I can only pray that God will give you courage and wisdom, because what you write, and how you write it, will have an important bearing on the future of our beloved country.

28. The Black Journalist and the Black Community

How is it possible to say that David Livingstone discovered the Victoria Falls? Weren't there people who had seen the Falls, perhaps every day of their lives, before Livingstone's so-called discovery? It was a discovery for *whites*, and history was written to fit in with their world view.

I am saying that you have an obligation to give the truth, and nothing but the truth, but from a black perspective. I also believe that you have an obligation to work for the liberation of our people. You must be involved in the Black Consciousness Movement, which seeks to remind blacks of their tremendous heritage as the children of God, that they are not faint carbon copies of others, but are each a glorious original, that they are of immense and indeed infinite value in the sight of God.

I remember vividly how I was inspired as a youngster by reading the black American journal 'Ebony'. It warmed the cockles of my heart, as I contemplated the odds against achieving anything worthwhile, reading about those brothers and sisters in the US, who had made it, also against daunting odds. I didn't know anything about baseball then, but I thrilled at Jackie Robinson's achievement of breaking into the major league, by playing for what were then called the Brooklyn Dodgers. How many of us grew inches because of films such as 'Stormy Weather'? I don't think it was particularly memorable, but it had an all black cast, and wasn't that something in those far off days?

You have a tremendous role to play in lauding black achievement, and telling our people that we *can* make it against all kinds of odds, and that the sky is the limit. We must be proud of you—so they can't say, 'We told you so—these blacks are irresponsible.' In your failure we all fail. If you succeed—'Oh he is exceptional.' Never mind. Don't fail us. You wield something they reckon is stronger than the sword—the pen. South Africa spent R.64,000,000 because she thought so to some extent.

29. An Easter Message

NOTHING COULD have been deader than Jesus on the Cross on that first Good Friday. And the hopes of his disciples had appeared to die with his crucifixion. Nothing could have been deeper than the despair of his followers when they saw their Master hanging on the Cross like a common criminal. The darkness that covered the earth for three hours during that Friday symbolised the blackness of their despair.

And then Easter happened. Jesus rose from the dead. The incredible, the unexpected happened. Life triumphed over death, light over darkness, love over hatred, good over evil. That is what Easter means—hope prevails over despair. Jesus reigns as Lord of Lords and King of Kings. Oppression and injustice and suffering can't be the end of the human story. Freedom and justice, peace and reconciliation, are his will for all of us, black and white, in this land and throughout the world. Easter says to us that despite everything to the contrary, his will for us will prevail, love will prevail over hate, justice over injustice and oppression, peace over exploitation and bitterness.

The Lord is risen. Alleluia.

Part Four

Freedom is Coming

30. The Certainty of Freedom

The text of an article, dated 8 November 1978.

WE OFTEN hear it said that people learn from history—not to repeat the mistakes of the past and to benefit from the experience of others. But a cynic, looking at our sorry record, declared: 'We learn from history that we don't learn from history.' There is much evidence to support that remark. We have a wonderful capacity for self-deception. When we are driving along our roads we see the wrecks that lie about our roadsides—cars that for one reason or another have come to grief. Almost always we tell ourselves that that could not happen to me—it always happens to others, doesn't it?

I write in this vein to set the backdrop to my belief—that the liberation and freedom of the blacks in this land are inevitable. And the liberation of blacks involves the liberation of the whites in our beloved country, because until blacks are free, the whites can never be really free. There is no such thing as separate freedom freedom is indivisible. At the present time we see our white fellow South Africans investing much of their resources to protect their so-called separate freedoms and privileges. They have little time left to enjoy them as they check the burglar proofing, the alarm system, the gun under the pillow and the viciousness of the watchdog. These resources could be employed in more creative ways to improve the quality of life of the entire community. Our white fellow South Africans think that their security lies in possessing a formidable and sophisticated arsenal of weapons. But they must know in their hearts that the security of all of us consists in a population whose members, black and white, are reasonably contented because they share more equitably in the good things of life, which all, black and white, have co-operated to produce.

So why do I believe that black liberation is inevitable? Or to put it another way: 'Why do I believe that real change, not just cosmetic change, is inevitable?' I believe this to be so because even the government thinks it must happen. Long ago, oh so long ago, we were told that South Africa was moving away from discrimination based on race. Nearly everybody is agreed that change is necessary. The former Prime Minister, Mr Vorster, saw this so clearly that he declared that if it did not happen, we would all be faced with the alternative too ghastly to contemplate.

But more fundamentally, I believe history teaches us a categorical lesson: that once a people are determined to become free, then nothing in the world can stop them reaching their goal. In the eighteenth century, Great Britain enjoyed a hegemony that extended to what came to be called the New World. She ruled over the thirteen Colonies of North America, as their Mother Country. These Colonies began to chafe at the bit, to find their colonial status galling. They had heard a British Parliamentarian pleading the case for their independence, and proclaiming: 'Taxation without representation is tyranny.' When their appeals for self-determination appeared to fall on deaf ears, then the thirteen Colonies, these puny things, threw the gauntlet down to the intimidating British Empire. The struggle seemed wholly unequal, but in the end, the thirteen Colonies emerged victorious against formidable odds. Nobody would have thought that when they signed their Declaration of Independence on 4 July 1776, that the thirteen Colonies would emerge the victors, thereby laying the foundation for the present day United States of America.

There are many other examples from history. France, through the French Revolution with its slogan of Liberty, Fraternity and Equality, when the exploited, against all the odds, overturned an oppressive system. In modern times we have had the Civil Rights movement in the USA, and the emergence out of colonial bondage of the so-called Dark Continent. Then there was the extraordinary resistance of the peasant people of Vietnam, who frustrated the efforts first of France, and then, incredibly, of the most powerful nation in the world—the USA—who were made to bite the dust in this struggle for the right to self-determination of a small people. My last reference is from the history of the Afrikaners. They believed themselves to be victims of British exploitation and musunderstanding. And we know what eventually happened. They triumphed so that today they are at the pinnacle of their power.

It seems, therefore, to be a universal law that when a people decide to become free, then absolutely nothing will eventually prevent them from reaching their goal. Why should it be thought that we blacks in South Africa will prove the exceptions to this rule?

For those among our people who feel despondent and hopeless, I want to assert that we shall be free. Do not despair of this. We shall be free because our cause is a just cause. We do not want to dominate others. We just want to have our humanity acknowledged. Our freedom is not in the gift of the white people. They cannot decide to give or to withold it. Our freedom is an inalienable right bestowed on us by God. And the God whom we worship has always shown himself to be one who takes sides. He is a God who opposes evil and injustice and oppression. He is a God who sides with those who are oppressed because he is that kind of God, and not because the oppressed are morally better than their oppressors. And in setting at liberty the oppressed and exploited, he will also set free those who are enslaved by their human sinfulness. Let us rejoice. Let us lift up our heads and straighten our drooping shoulders. God cares and God will act decisively to bring justice, peace and reconciliation in our land. We will walk, black and white together, into this new South Africa, where people will matter because they are persons of infinite value, created in the image of God, the liberator God.

31. The Black Mood Today

The Silverton raid was an ANC operation—an attack on a bank— that developed into a siege during which three ANC men were killed.

A FEW weeks ago one of the gunmen involved in the Silverton Raid was buried in Soweto. 15,000 people attended the funeral—most of whom were young blacks. Their perceptions were quite different from those of most whites, who regarded the dead man as a terrorist—the blacks honoured him and his companions as heroes. I am sure those who attended the funeral knew they would have to run the gauntlet of squads of policemen; that they might have their eyes smarting from teargas, and that they might well have to escape the snapping jaws of vicious police dogs. And yet they came in their thousands, with clenched fists beating against the skies, and their throats pouring forth what we call our freedom songs. 'Let them leave alone our land.' 'God give us strength, give us strength not to fear, give us strength because we need it.'

I want to point out something most whites and quite a few black adults do not yet know. And it is this. We really have a new breed of black exemplified by the young people who turned up at the funeral of the Silverton gunman. We of an older generation are on the whole still scared of arrest, of police dogs, of teargas, of prison and of deaths. But these young people are quite something else. They have experienced it all—yes, they have seen friends, brothers and sisters die and they are no longer scared. They are just determined. They are determined that they are going to be free, they and their reluctant cowed parents. They have, they believe, sat for too long, listening night after night to the stories of their parents' daily humiliations just because they were black. They have decided that enough is enough, and so they are people with iron in their souls. They are determined with a new kind of determination. Most of them believe that the goal which they are determined to reach—true liberation in what they call a united Azania—can come only with bloodshed and violence. They say this, and that is what is so shocking, in a matter of fact kind of way, for they say their leaders have tried everything peaceful and they have nothing to show for their efforts.

The determination of these young people has rubbed off on their parents, who are becoming politicised by so many things—the growing frustration with unemployment, the long queues to get 'influxed', the humiliation of pass raids, the inequities of the educational system, the travel on overcrowded buses and trains—one could go on much longer with this litany of woe. They too are getting more angry as they see so much wealth existing cheek by jowl with their poverty, and Mr Mugabe's victory in Zimbabwe has had an electrifying effect on blacks—most of whom whooped with real joy when they saw the goal of freedom being achieved. They are wondering how long they can go on believing change will come peacefully, when all the evidence seems to point in the other direction. The country is becoming more effectively armed, the authorities take action against all real leaders who want peaceful change, the pass laws are being more strictly applied, and many people are still being moved out to starve in the 'homelands'. There is bitterness and anger and hatred, which could easily develop into an all engulfing explosion.

Two years ago I spoke at Pietermaritzburg about reasonably peaceful change. After the meeting a black youngster, about twelve years old, said 'Father, I heard what you said, do you believe it?' I said 'Yes, though sometimes I hold on to this belief by the skin of my teeth.' He replied: 'Show me what you have achieved with all your talk of peaceful change, and I will show you what we gained with just a little violence.'

I will give one more example of the determination amongst our young black people. Some time ago I appeared in mitigation in a court in Pretoria. The accused—twelve people were on trial for allegedly taking part in military training—had asked that Revd Buti or I should come to plead in mitigation for them. Revd Buti was unable to go, so I was greatly privileged to appear instead. I say greatly privileged advisedly, as you will hear.

Some of the accused were young, and they had spent nearly sixteen months in custody. We don't know what was done to them during that time, but part of that time was spent in the maximum security section of Pretoria prison. This is the section that contains the death cells, which are hardly empty as far as blacks are concerned. So I thought I would see people who had had the stuffing knocked out of them. And on that morning six of them who had been found guilty, knew that the hangman's noose was hanging over their heads. But what did we find? Just before the judge came in it was these accused who were the most vivacious people in the court.

One of the accused said this in his statement, before sentence was passed. 'Your Lordship, I went into this with my eyes open. I have a vision of a new South Africa, where people count because they are human, and where the colour of one's skin is irrelevant. The tragedy is that it will cost so much to bring this South Africa about. I am young and recently married; we have one child. I would like to be with my wife and have more children. But I am ready to accept whatever penalty you wish to impose on me. I may not enjoy this new South Africa, but my brother will.'

32. The Impact of the Soweto Riots

The riots in the township of Soweto, five miles from Johannesburg, caused widespread unease amongst the white population. On 16 June 1976, thousands of schoolchildren marched against a decree ordering an increase in the use of Afrikaans in schools. Rioting, which spread through South Africa, broke out when police shot thirteen-year-old Hector Peterson in the back. About 500 young black people were killed in the troubles, which lasted from June 1976 to January 1977.

MANY COMMENTATORS, when asked to give their assessment of the South African situation after 16 June 1976, replied with a well-worn cliche: 'South Africa will never be the same again.' It is a hackneyed expression, but it has been proved to be only too true by subsequent events.

Before that fateful day most of us declared that anybody trained in the Bantu education system, could be little other than a docile, unthinking conformist. We did not think they were capable of protesting in such a disciplined manner. And yet it was precisely those children, who had been fed on the thin gruel that passed for education, who said in no uncertain terms: 'We have had enough. We are God's children made in his image, and we demand our birthright of an educational system equal to that for children of other racial groups in South Africa.'

Yes, those children took everyone by surprise, including their own parents. Even the Security Police, who have riddled our community with a network of informers, were caught with their pants down—quite unprepared for what the children had decided to do. We now know that the issues of education, and the attempted imposition of the Afrikaans language, were merely the immediate causes of the students' anger. Their protest meant that they rejected the entire apartheid system of legalised inferiority, oppression, injustice and exploitation. They were saying: 'We belong to South Africa, and we are going to have our rightful share of all her resources—social, political, economic and eduational. We are not going to apologise for our existence. God did not make a mistake in creating us black, and we are going to participate in all the forms of decision making—especially political—which affect our lives. Nothing is going to stop us becoming free; our freedom is a gift from God and not something that whites can withold or grant as they wish.'

That message has gone the length and breadth of our beautiful and beloved land. Four years later it was taken up by so-called Coloureds protesting against a third class citizenship. Now there is this new determination abroad. All blacks (Indians, Coloureds, Africans) know they are all oppressed. You can't have a woman who is half pregnant. You are either oppressed or privileged. So we have a new solidarity to add to the determination that we shall all be free, black and white together, and nothing but just nothing can stop us. There are many who would suffer imprisonment, exile or even death to attain the glorious goal of true freedom for all in a united South Africa. We are called to work for true freedom and liberation for all—otherwise we will perish in the alternative too ghastly to contemplate.

Nkosi sikelel' iAfrika—Morena Boloka sechaba sa heso (God bless Africa). Let it be so (Makubenjalo). Yes, South Africa can never be the same again, because of what happened on 16 June 1976.

33. Free Nelson Mandela

Nelson Mandela, imprisoned since 1962 on Robben island, is the leader of the ANC. Born in 1918, he worked as a lawyer in Johannesburg, and led the Defiance Campaign against Unjust Laws of 1952. He was put on trial in 1956 for treason, with 155 others, but everyone was eventually acquitted in 1960. After Sharpeville he went underground, and became known as the 'Black Pimpernel', continuing to organise in South Africa. He went abroad in 1962, to try and gain support from African heads of state and politicians in London. But soon after he returned to South Africa he was arrested and sentenced to five years for inciting strikes, and leaving the country without a valid passport. Following a police raid on the secret ANC Headquarters in Rivonia—a district of Johannesburg—he was taken from his cell, to face trial with eight others on charges of sabotage, and conspiracy to overthrow the government. One man was acquitted, but the eight men found guilty, including Mandela, were sentenced to life imprisonment on Robben Island. At the time of writing, he has been in prison for nearly twenty years.

This is the text of an address delivered at Natal University on 28 April 1980.

MY OPINION is that we are going to have a black Prime Minister in South Africa within the next five-to-ten years. No serious minded person today thinks that it is possible for a group outnumbered five to one, as the white community is by blacks, can go on forever lording it over the majority. All the logic of history is against such a thing happening.

Also, recent years have seen significant developments in the white community in South Africa. We used to think that the

Afrikaner community, which has produced our rulers, was a monolithic, immovable structure, which would resist any efforts to reduce its power as a united group. That is not the case any longer. There are unprecedented rumblings within the Afrikaans Church; the very Church which has always provided the religious and moral justification for the existence of the Afrikaner community. There is no longer that awesome solidarity and unanimity within the religious manifestation of the Afrikaner community.

The Information Scandal ('Muldergate') shook many of the more principled members of the Afrikaans community. For some it was not merely disillusioning, it was positively traumatic; shaking the foundations of their belief that though their policies might sometimes cause hurt, they were basically morally justifiable. It could be that once they realise that apartheid can no longer be justified scripturally, that they throw caution to the winds, saying any method that ensures their survival is justified. It could also be that if they were threatened by a common foe, they would all rush into the laager. But what I am trying to stress is that we no longer have a united mass, which knows where it is going or how to get there. That will have significant political consequences.

Do I need to point out that the Afrikaner psyche has also been shaken by Afrikaans writers and literary men, who, with apparent intransigence, have declared that they find censorship intolerable? What about the Afrikaans press, which has been heard to say that whites must be ready to share what they have, or risk losing it all? Or even saying that the authorities should speak to the *real* leaders of the black community. This is a different kind of Afrikaans community, slightly more awake as disaster stares them in the face. We should not get too enthusiastic, but these are the pointers to the changes occurring in Afrikanerdom.

The Prime Minister has been saying things that we would not have expected from a Nationalist Prime Minister. He has been saying 'Adapt or die', and he is a realist, who has been told by his military advisors that there is no way the white community can win a war, conventional or unconventional, with 80% of the population disaffected. I have concentrated on the Afrikaners for the simple reason that they hold the key to political power, and that in the end the discussion is going to have to be between the Afrikaners and the blacks.

Blacks may not have much military power. But we have our consumer power, and South Africa still depends to a large extent on our labour. We are not yet properly organised, but the latent power is there. Banning, detentions, banishments will not stop freedom coming. They merely postpone the inevitable, and build up a legacy of bitterness and hatred, which we could well do without, as we learned from Zimbabwe. Okay—there is going to be a black Prime Minister in South Africa within five-to-ten years. The white community cannot stop that happening. What the white community still has in its power to do is to decide whether that Prime Minister is going to end up there through a process of reasoned negotiation, and discussion at a conference table, or whether he will have to do so after bitter fighting and bloodshed. I think we have a very good chance of pulling off the first alternative. And we need Nelson Mandela, because he is almost certainly going to be that first black Prime Minister. He represents all our genuine leaders, in prison and in exile. So to call for his release is really to say, please let us sit down, black and white together, each with our acknowledged leaders, and work out our common future, so that we can move into this new South Africa, which will be filled with justice, peace, love, righteousness, compassion and caring.

One would like to say to some politicians: 'learn at least one lesson from Zimbabwe—don't make such categorical statements. You will have to eat your words—look at Mr Ian Smith and his "no black majority rule in a 1000 years".' It is possible that some politicians will end up being totally irrelevant. Retirement might do some of them good.

God loves us in South Africa very dearly. He has said, I want to give you an object lesson on how *not* to solve a political crisis—and he has unfolded before us the lesson of Zimbabwe. They could have been at this point in their history without the price of over 20,000 deaths, devastation, bitterness and hatred which they have had to pay. I think we can have a new non-racial South Africa, and that we can achieve it reasonably peacefully, but that means we must negotiate and bargain at the conference table, and this can only be done by genuine and acknowledged leaders. Hence our call, Free Mandela, and start talking.

34. Black Consumer Power—One lever for Change

In addition to the power that blacks have as consumers, is the power of their labour, upon which South African prosperity is built. In recent years there has been a growth of trades unions amongst the black workforce, that has gained substantial support. The strike of the Municipal workers of Johannesburg in 1980, when the entire workforce came out for more pay, was a sign that the new unions were making themselves felt, and could play an important role in bringing about a more just society.

This has been taken from an address given at the opening of the Black Chain Supermarket, Johannesburg, 16 February 1980.

TODAY WE have come to say 'thank you God', thank you for a black achievement. I want to underline black. I do so because there are many in our country, both black and white, who still believe that black people are not quite able to do these things. You often hear them say, if a black has succeeded, 'Ah well, he is exceptional.' And if a black fails, then they will say, almost with glee: 'What did you expect — I told you so.' But we have come here to thank God for this black achievement.

Our people should know their consumer power. Many businesses in Johannesburg would collapse if we withdrew our support. Many white newspapers, such as the *Rand Daily Mail* or the *Sunday Times*, would have their circulation drastically reduced if blacks stopped buying them. Many building societies and banks would feel a cold draught if we withdrew our savings. And yet they still often treat us as if *they* were doing us favours. For a long time blacks have not been able to get housing loans from building societies—yet our money has helped to subsidise white housing. The building societies and banks could have agitated for a change in the law long ago, like the wine farmers, who insisted that blacks should be allowed to drink the so-called white man's liquor.

We have to realise our consumer power, and let white South Africa know about it, so that they negotiate with us as those who have that power. Some of these newspapers I have mentioned report news that affects us—as if we did not form an important part of their readership! They write as if their readers were only white. We should ask them to consider for instance their use of the term 'terrorist', when there are neutral terms they could use. We should remind them that they get advertising because of their circulation figures, and that black readership boosts these figures. We want fundamental change in South Africa reasonably peacefully—let these newspapers and businesses urge their government to negotiate with blacks before it is too late, because blacks have power.

You businessmen must succeed in this venture for the sake of black liberation, which involves white liberation as well. As long as blacks are not free, no one will be free in South Africa. Freedom is indivisible. You business people must realise that you won't prosper if you think only of yourselves. Our poor and unemployed and unprosperous blacks will drag you back. We must move forward together. Our prosperity must be one we share with the black community—after all, if you help to increase our buying power you end up with busy tills. You must be concerned with the betterment of our people—giving scholarships for education, helping cultural and other projects, being involved in community development projects—for the sake of all of us in South Africa. I believe in an undivided South Africa where we all matter because God has created us in his image. He has planned us even before we were conceived. We are each a VSP—a very special person.

35. My Vision for South Africa

From an article dated 25 March 1979.

WE SHOULD all have the freedom to become fully human. That is basic to my understanding of society—that God created us without any coercion, freely for freedom. Responsibility is a nonsense except in the context of freedom—freedom to accept or reject alternative options, freedom to obey or disobey. God, who alone has the perfect right to be a totalitarian, has such a tremendous respect for our freedom to be human, that he would much rather see us go freely to hell than compel us to go to heaven.

According to the Bible, a human being can be a human being only because he belongs to a community. A person is a person through other persons, as we say in our African idiom. And so separation of persons because of biological accidents is reprehensible and blasphemous. A person is entitled to a stable community life, and the first of these communities is the family. A stable family life would be of paramount importance in my South Africa.

There would be freedom of association, of thought and of expression. This would involve freedom of movement as well. One would be free to go wherever one wanted, to associate with whomsoever one wished. As adult humans we would not be subject to draconian censorship laws. We can surely decide for ourselves what we want to read, what films to view and what views to have. We must not be frogmarched into puritanism.

Because we are created in the image of God one of our attributes is creativity. South Africa is starved of the great things many of her children can create and do, because of artificial barriers, and the refusal to let people develop to their fullest potential. When one has been overseas and seen for example the Black Alvin Abbey dance group, which performed modern ballet to standing room only crowds at Covent Garden, then one weeps for how South Africa has allowed herself to be cheated of such performances by her own inhabitants. How many potentially outstanding people are being denied the opportunity to get on?

When I think of the splendid young people I have met, who despite some horrendous experiences at the hands of the system, have emerged· quite unscathed with bitterness, and who have a tremendous humanity and compassion, then I weep because we are so wantonly wasteful of human resources. We need a course on human ecology.

I lay great stress on humaneness and being truly human. In our African understanding, part of Ubantu—being human—is the rare gift of sharing. This concept of sharing is exemplified at African feasts even to this day, when people eat together from a common dish, rather than from individual dishes. That means a meal is indeed to have communion with one's fellows. Blacks are beginning to lose this wonderful attribute, because we are being inveigled by the excessive individualism of the West. I loathe Capitalism because it gives far too great play to our inherent selfishness. We are told to be highly competitive, and our children start learning the attitudes of the ratrace quite early. They mustn't just do well at school—they must sweep the floor with their rivals. That's how you get on. We give prizes to such persons, not so far as I know to those who know how best to get on with others, or those who can coax the best out of others. We must delight in our ulcers, the symbols of our success.

So I would look for a socio-economic system that placed the emphasis on sharing and giving, rather than on self-aggrandise-ment and getting. Capitalism is exploitative and I can't stand that. We need to engage the resources that each person has. My vision includes a society that is more compassionate and caring, in which 'superfluous appendages' (*the government's way of describing families of black workers*—Ed.) are unthinkable, where young and old are made to feel wanted, and that they belong and are not resented. It is a distorted community that trundles its aged off into soulless institutions. We need their accumulated wisdom and experience. They are splendid for helping the younger to feel cared for; certainly that has been the experience in the extended family.

I believe too that in a future South Africa we must be supportive of the family. The nuclear family is not geared to stand all the strains placed on it by modern day pressures. There are things we can survive better in a group than singly. I know there are pressures in the extended family, but I need to be persuaded that these are greater than those presently haunting the nuclear family.

Basically I long and work for a South Africa that is more open and more just; where people count and where they will have equal access to the good things of life, with equal opportunity to live, work, and learn. I long for a South Africa where there will be equal and untrammelled access to the courts of the land, where detention without trial will be a thing of the hoary past, where bannings and other such arbitrary acts will no longer be even so much as mentioned, and where the rule of law will hold sway in the fullest sense. In addition, all adults will participate fully in political decision making, and in other decisions which affect their lives. Consequently they will have the vote and be eligible for election to all public offices. This South Africa will have integrity of territory with a common citizenship, and all the rights and privileges that go with such a citizenship, belonging to all its inhabitants

Clearly, for many people, what I have described is almost a Utopia, and we cannot reach that desired goal overnight. Black leaders would, I feel, be willing to go back to the black community, and say: 'Hold on—things are moving in the right direction' if certain minimum conditions were pledged and met, even in stages, by the white powers that be. These are:

(A) Abolition of the Pass Laws.
(B) The immediate halting of population removals.
(C) The scrapping of Bantu Education, and a move towards a unitary educational system.
(D) A commitment to call a National Convention.

These would be significant steps towards realising the vision.

Part Five

The Challenge of the Eighties

36. Survival as a Human Society

Though the population explosion question has dropped out of the limelight, that does not mean the problem is over. According to Professor Robert May, Professor of Biology at Princeton, 'The global population of human beings is increasing now, if anything, faster than it was ten years ago, when it was a fashionable thing to be worried about.' By the end of the century, it is estimated that global population will have increased from the current level of 4.5 billion, up to 6 billion people.

WE STAND at the beginning of a new decade that must surely be a crucial one for our survival as a human society. We have been warned often enough. When one reads books such as Toffler's 'Future Shock' or the Club of Rome's 'Limits to Growth', one wishes that the future they predict would not come upon us. Their prognostications are so bleak and unattractive. We are warned that unless we take drastic action now, then we will have had it. They tell us that we face the danger of being overwhelmed by vast numbers, because of the approaching population explosion. There is, after all, only so much space available, and this space can accommodate only so many people at an optimum level of existence. Apart from the likely disappearance of space to house all the teeming millions that are likely to people the earth by the turn of the century, we are being warned that there is no way in which the earth will be able to produce enough food for all its inhabitants.

We have not been responsible stewards of our land resources; we have pillaged and plundered as if we could replenish the irreplaceable topsoil, that has been ravaged by wasteful agricultural methods. The earth's surface is being desecrated at an alarming rate.

As if that were not already serious enough, we are wantonly wasteful of our non-replenishable fossil fuel resources—our coal and oil and gas stockpiles are not inexhaustible. And whilst some may look hopefully at nuclear energy, we have been warned about the hazards of tampering with it—note the recent near disaster at the Harrisburg nuclear station in the USA. Moreover, nobody has yet come up with a solution to the problem of the disposal of nuclear waste, waste that has a long radio-active life.

Have you had enough? What about the threat of the mushroom cloud? We look on helplessly as country after country attains nuclear capability. We see the mad scramble of the arms race, the investment of scarce capital resources that could have been used in socially beneficial schemes.

There is an uneasy global equilibrium. The earth has perhaps never been more vulnerable than it appears to be in our day. The uneasy truce is always in grave danger of being broken, especially as we notice the gap between the affluent West (including Japan) and the poor so-called Third World. The gap is widening and augurs ill for the peace of the world. Our earth home is, it seems, always on the edge of a conflagration.

37. Future Challenges: South Africa

The South African Prime Minister, Mr Botha, fought the 1981 white only election to gain a mandate for his policy of peripheral reforms to the apartheid system. These reforms, such as the international hotels mentioned (where black and white people can drink in the same bars) leave the structure of apartheid untouched, and go nowhere near to satisfying black aspirations in South Africa.

THERE CAN be no doubt at all that the most serious challenge facing the world today is not Communism, despite the adventures of Soviet Russia in Afghanistan, which have given South Africa a temporary breathing space. Most of the Westerners who have tended to have an obsession with the threat of world domination

106

posed by Communism, would like us to believe that that is in fact the case. South Africa has capitalised on this by describing herself, and trying to project herself, as the last bastion of Christian Western Civilisation, against the predatory advances of Communism. It has passed such laws as the Suppression of Communism Act and other viciously repressive legislation, and many in the West have been duped. 'Communist' in South Africa has become the favourite swearword of those who support apartheid and the Nationalist government. Any opponent of apartheid could fall foul of the Suppression of Communism Act, even if he was known to be an ordained minister of a Christian denomination, who believed in God and who worshipped regularly. Very few in South Africa care to point out the blatant contradiction in all this.

We have had to tell our white fellow South Africans that for blacks, the immediate concern is not with Communism, however defined. For us it is but a future and hypothetical threat. Our priority concern as blacks, is the harsh reality of the present, which we experience every day of our lives at nearly every point. Our humanity is denigrated, called into question, and determined by an arbitrary criterion for which we cannot be praised or blamed—the colour of our skins. Our priority concern is that we are treated as less than third-grade citizens in the land of our birth, in an effort to keep political power in the hands of a small white oligarchy outnumbered five to one. It is a system of institutionalised violence, using migratory labour, which *deliberately*, not accidentally, destroys black family life. It is a system that uses structural unemployment, by having reservoirs of unskilled labour in the 'homelands', to provide cheap labour. It uses the institutionalised violence of forced population removals to keep black people in their place. Human beings are uprooted from areas where they have normally had adequate housing, and work of some sort, to be dumped as if they were sacks of potatoes in some God-forsaken arid area, many times without adequate alternative accommodation. They are usually too far from places of work, and so they sit there listlessly, 'waiting to die', as some of them have said.

They are sent to these resettlement camps to starve. It is not accidental. It is part of the government policy to remove the blacks from so-called white South Africa, so that these blacks can exercise their political rights in a soapbox opera land, with a spurious independence recognised only by white South Africa. This is done so that the whites can say that blacks have no claim to political representation in 'white' South Africa, because they are all aliens there.

I visited several of these resettlement camps. At one of them I saw a little girl, who lived with her widowed mother and sister, and asked,

'Does your mother get a pension or a grant?'
'No,' she replied.
'Then what do you do for food?'
'We borrow food,' she replied.
'Have you ever returned any of the food that you have borrowed?'
'No.'
'What do you do when you can't borrow food?'
'We drink water to fill our stomachs.'

That happens in a land that boasts that it can send maize to starving Zambia. This is the policy of apartheid, and that is how it intends to solve the political crisis in our land. *That* is the real challenge that stares the world in the face in the 1980s. What are you going to do about South Africa, which follows such an inhumane, such an evil and diabolical policy? I have already warned in South Africa that if the government are determined to go ahead with their population uprooting schemes, and their policy of depriving blacks of their South African citizenship, then we can kiss goodbye to any hopes of a reasonably peaceful solution, for which I and many others are working. We will be embroiled in a bloodbath, or what former Prime Minister of South Africa, Mr Vorster, called 'the alternative too ghastly to contemplate'.

There are only two options left for South Africa. One is for the white minority to hold on to all political power, making minor and peripheral adjustments—this leads as inexorably to violence and bloodshed as night follows day, and we must do everything to avert that national suicide. The other is that they agree that their salvation and true security lie in political power-sharing—this can still happen. Of course it will mean a declension in the very high standard of living that white South Africa enjoys. But we say they should be willing to give up something, rather than risk losing everything. Let them negotiate whilst they can do so from a position of strength, and whilst there are those amongst the blacks who still want to negotiate for a reasonably peaceful settlement. Every day that passes merely serves to erode further the credibility of those wanting to talk, and increase the acceptability of those who say the only language possible is the language of force.

The United Nations has declared that the apartheid system poses a threat to world peace. This would include the unresolved situation in Namibia. What I am saying is that if a racial war were to erupt in South Africa, it could very well trigger off a Third World War. This is not being melodramatic, because we saw how the United States and the Soviet Union were in an eyeball to eyeball confrontation over Angola. South Africa is a much more coveted prize. In addition, as a senior US Senator told me in Washington DC, a racial upheaval in South Africa would have the most horrendous consequences for race relations in the USA. This would apply certainly also to Britain, where race relations are already on the boil. One might point out that several Western countries have significant concentrations of people from Third World countries. So the situation in those countries would not be left untouched by a South African racial explosion.

However, one knows that many Westerners, and this sadly includes their churches, are really loath to take decisive action against South Africa, action to ensure that there was a rapid evolution to majority rule. (Not *black* but *majority* rule.) In part it is because their kith and kin are involved, so they are affected in emotional ways. The West is also involved financially, so it feels that change could threaten their investments. They are embroiled

109

with South Africa through military and especially nuclear collaboration (though they deny this vehemently). So one questions whether there is a real will to see fundamental change happening, without bloodshed and through the armed struggle. I am still hoping that we can persuade our Western brothers and sisters to exert all the diplomatic, political and economic pressure possible, to drive us to the conference table. But I sense a great deal of reluctance to exert this pressure, and too much enthusiasm to refer to changes that are supposedly happening under the Botha administration.

Mr P. W. Botha has a greater grasp of reality than most of his predecessors. But apartheid is not dead; we have not seen the corpse, or been invited to the funeral. People speak about changes in the sports arena, in so-called international hotels, in restaurants and cinemas which allow blacks admission together with whites, and of the removal of discriminatory signs. The best that can be said about all this is that they probably create a climate for change, and begin a process which it might be difficult to reverse. But most blacks see these as cosmetic, superficial changes, which do nothing for those who live in ghettos and travel in overcrowded trains and buses to and from work.

It is possible that the government may be beginning a new strategy, of doing away with discrimination based on race alone. It may be ready to co-opt some blacks, with substantial material privileges, who will then act as a buffer middle-class between the whites and the have-not blacks, and who will become vociferous supporters of the status quo that gives them so many privileges. It will then cease being just a race question. It will have become a class struggle. But social and economic concessions and privileges, however substantial, are always vulnerable since they depend on the whim of those who possess political power.

So surely the most immediate, most urgent, challenge for the 1980s is South Africa, until a more just and open non-racial society exists in that beautiful land.

38. The Affluent West and the Third World

'What are you Freedom?
You are clothes and fire and food . . .
And a neat and happy home . . .
For the trampled multitudes.'

(Verse adapted from 'The Masque of Anarchy', P. B. Shelley, 1819)

Colonial powers restructured the economies of many Third World countries by gearing them up for cash-crops for export, at the expense of the food crops for the indigenous populations. This still continues, and the developing countries have little control over the prices charged for their raw materials. The price of cotton, for example, is fixed in New York, and it is the transnational corporations which control prices and distribution of the poorer countries' raw materials. This system must be changed if Third World countries are ever to receive a fair price for their goods; on some transactions they get as little as 2% of the eventual retail price.

The global death toll from starvation amounts to 30 million people every year, and in Asia, Africa and South America there is serious deprivation in rural areas, which leads to people moving away to overcrowded, insanitary and burgeoning shanty towns on the edges of major cities. Food production therefore declines further, so the building up of prosperity, and a viable life with decent facilities for the people in these rural areas is a priority.

'To meet their needs' say George McRobie and Marilyn Carr, in Mass Production or Production by the Masses?, 'a new technology must be discovered or devised; one that lies, as it were, between the sickle and the combine harvester . . .' They point out that 'all the pressures of the past 100 years . . . have been towards labour saving, capital-intensive, highly centralised methods of production. What we now need most urgently is a new set of technologies, designed by *people who are informed by the need to develop capital saving technologies—capable of being decentralised to the maximum extent.' In other words, the approach is to 'find out what people are trying to do, and help them to do it better.'*

I WOULD place, as next on the agenda, the growing gap between the affluent, developed countries mainly found in the Northern hemisphere, and the abject poverty of the developing countries, found mainly in the Southern hemisphere. In the latter are to be found two-thirds of the world's inhabitants, who enjoy an infinitesimal percentage of the wealth of the globe we inhabit. There is a harshness in the rapacity of the industrialised giants, as they play havoc with ecology in their wanton exploitation of the resources of the earth. The wealthy consume a great deal more than can be justified by their population figures. But it will not be that the hungry masses will forever just look on at the groaning tables of their wealthy neighbours. This could be the next flashpoint. We from Africa will have to raise this question in international forums. We must call for a more equitable distribution and sharing of the good things of the earth, fair prices for our primary products, and more just competition in the markets of the world. I have no doubt that many who come from the poorer parts of the world have grown somewhat cynical about the so-called free enterprise system. In it some are certainly a great deal freer than others. From my perspective Capitalism seems to give unbridled license to human cupidity, and has a morality that belongs properly to the jungle—'the survival of the fittest, the weakest to the wall, and the devil take the hindmost'. I find what I have seen of Capitalism and the free enterprise system quite morally repulsive. I long for a society which is not so grasping, not ruled by the laws of the ratrace, but one in which there is more sharing. I deplore the sort of society which is uncaring and selfish, and hope that we will work for a society that is more compassionate and caring, and values people not because they are consumers or producers, but because they are of infinite value, since they are created in the image of God.

112

So the second major challenge is posed by the gap between the rich developed world, and the vastly poorer developing world. If we are not careful it could be that starved men and women will march on empty stomachs, to invade the well-stocked larders of the wealthy. Desperate people use desperate methods. We will die as fools, if we cannot learn to live together as brothers—to paraphrase Martin Luther King.

39. A Prophetic Church and Human Rights in the Third World

Archbishop Luwum was murdered in Uganda in February 1977, on the orders of Idi Amin, after he had presented a written petition on the question of human rights, which were being flagrantly violated with torture, murder and rape being practised by Amin's army.

THE CHURCH in Africa, and the Church in the Third World generally, must come into its own. We know that the Church took a risky turn at the time of Constantine's conversion, when it became a licit organisation, allied with the State and the powerful. It did not always maintain a critical distance, so that it could carry out its prophetic ministry and say: 'Thus saith the Lord. . . .' The result was that the poor and the voiceless found themselves opposed by the very body that should have been on their side. It was all too easy for the Church to sanctify an unjust status quo, because it stood to benefit materially from its alliance with the high and mighty, totally unmindful of its vocation to be a serving Church.

In the newly independent Third World countries, we have often seen serious inroads into civil liberties and human rights. The position of the people has often been worse under their own rulers, than it ever was under their colonial masters. There is often no freedom of speech, or press freedom. Criticism of the abuse of power by largely totalitarian military dictatorships, is frowned on.

113

Political dissent is not allowed, on the pretence that developing countries cannot afford the luxury of having a democratic system, or that one-party states are not necessarily dictatorships.

Unfortunately, there are very few such. One is worried that the lot of our Third World is such a hard one, with so few examples of peaceful transition from one set of political leaders to another. Corruption is rife, and the people, in their already impoverished condition, have to bear the brunt of all this. My worry is that the Church has by and large been too quiescent, seemingly afraid to rock the boat too much. There are splendid and glorious exceptions, such as Archbishop Luwum who confronted the evil Amin with the demands of the Gospel of Jesus Christ, and paid for this courageous act with his life—or the experience of Cardinal Malula in Zaire. My concern is for the integrity of the Church of Jesus Christ. We must be seen to be motivated, not by political considerations, but by the imperatives of the Gospel, speaking out that evil is evil, whether perpetrated by black or white. The Church must be willing to pay the price of its loyalty to its Lord and Master. Political leaders have often been let down by a sychophan-tic Church leadership, who should provide moral and ethical guidance, but who are content to be time-servers. The Church in Africa is faced with this challenge of injustice, corruption, oppression and exploitation at home, and it has no option but to fulfil its prophetic vocation, or seriously call in question its claim to be the Church of Jesus Christ. We in Africa have much to learn here from the Church in Latin America, and also in South Korea.

Related to this question of the role of the Church *vis-à-vis* governments, is its stand over the growing gap between the rich, who grow ever richer, and the poor who grow ever poorer in our countries. The rich Africans become expert exploiters of fellow Africans, and the Church is tempted to side with the rich and the powerful, ignoring the poor, those whom Christ called the least of His brethren. We must move into the slums that are rising so quickly around our cities, we must minister to the prostitute and the down and out. We must be the Church of the poor and the marginalised ones, who have no power or voice. We must become

114

their voice and strive to empower them, and help them help
themselves so that they can enter into their heritage—the heritage
of the freedom of the children of God, and a humanity that is
measured by nothing less than the humanity of Jesus Christ
Himself.

40. Divided Churches

*From a sermon preached at Bosmont, and an address on the subject of
Church unity.*

DURING THE 1970s I visited Northern Ireland; I had been invited to
address the General Assembly of the Presbyterian Church in
Ireland. Ulster, of course, has been wracked by a civil war between,
on the one side, Protestant groups who want to remain linked to
Britain, and who are the top dogs; on the other side there are the
Roman Catholics who want to be united with Eire, where they
would hope to enjoy a better deal than they do at present, as a
somewhat deprived minority. We have been told times without
number of the horrible casualties of this war—if you are a
Protestant in a Roman Catholic area then your days are usually
numbered and vice-versa. The brutality is often unbelievable.

While visiting that sadly divided land I was taken on a tour of
Belfast. On the surface things looked quite normal. People were
rushing to work, mothers were taking children to school, and
doing their shopping. It all looked quite normal, until one looked
at the buildings which had been gutted by fire, and the streets that
had been scarred by bombs. It all looked quite normal until one
saw the troop carriers, with soldiers holding guns, their fingers
always on the trigger—then that air of the normal became quite
eerie. I won't easily forget a particularly shattering sight which will

remain etched on my memory—it was almost as if it had been set up for my benefit. At one street corner were two groups of children and youngsters, obviously belonging to the two opposing sides in the strife. They were taunting one another and throwing stones at one another.

At one level this quarrel was political—a matter of civil rights for a minority—but at another level it was religious, because the two sides belonged, one to the Roman Catholic Church, and the other to the various Protestant denominations. And look at what Christianity has done to the children. They belong to a faith that claims that its Lord and Master had broken down the middle wall of partition, and made all people one as members of His body, the Church. But looking at those children, all the protestations about reconciliation sounded so hollow.

During the Assembly one of the delegates described a horrifying incident. He told of some teenage girls who had gone to drink at a pub, then went on to stone to death a girl belonging to the other side. After this cold-blooded murder they had returned to drink at the pub without showing the slightest remorse. That civil war has brutalised and dehumanised not only the adults, but the children also. What must Jesus feel when He looks down on us? He must surely weep as he wept for Jerusalem. It was gratifying to hear in that Assembly what efforts were being made by the Churches *together* to minister in that awful situation—how they were trying to heal the raw wounds of bigotry, hatred and bitterness, and how they were being drawn together through their common ministry, perhaps more effectively than through all the debates they had had about Church unity. The Churches must beat their breasts in deep penitence for their part in helping to divide God's children into warring camps, instead of being agents of unity and justice and reconciliation. The dividedness of the Churches makes it difficult for people to believe in the Gospel of Jesus Christ.

Divided Churches are ineffective and wasteful. If we could pool our resources, we would be far more effective. Is it not wantonly wasteful of God's resources that each denomination must for instance build its own church, so that in one area, say of Soweto,

116

there will be several church buildings belonging to rival denominations. Would it not be better to come together, and put up one or two structures which could be used by different denominations? The money saved could be used more effectively, to help feed the hungry, or to provide scholarships. It is a powerful argument—but it is ultimately not the real reason why the Christian Church should be one.

Some say the Churches are ineffective in their witness because they speak with many voices instead of one. When we met with the Prime Minister he said to what Church must he listen, since they all come to him, and speak differently when they do. President Samora Machel is reported to have told the Churches in Mozambique that he would listen to them only when they were united, speaking corporately and together. That again is a powerful argument, but it is not the real reason for our concern for Church unity.

The real reason is that our dividedness undermines the Gospel of Jesus Christ. He came to bring reconciliation; he broke down the middle wall of partition. How can we, the Church of God, say to a sadly divided world that we have the remedy for your animosities, your hatreds, your separateness, when we are ourselves so sinfully divided? Surely the world will retort, 'Physician heal thyself'. How can the Church, say in Northern Ireland, really preach reconciliation between the warring factions in that land, when Protestant and Roman Catholic are unable to share the bread of life together in Church?

What about us in South Africa? How can we say apartheid is evil and contrary to the Gospel of Love when we practise such a sad ecclesiastical apartheid? We have racially divided Churches, and we find all kinds of excuses to justify this. We say we are residentially segregated, or that there are language problems. We appoint our ministers on a racial basis. Whites can serve both black and white congregations, but only in the rarest situations have blacks ministered in white congregations. If they have done so, they have usually been assisted. Until recently our salaries were racially determined, and even now most of our multiracial

Churches are really run by the minority—the whites. We have reflected our unjust and discriminatory society. Those who have been and still are victims of the injustice and oppression of apartheid, have seen the Churches as part of the oppressive system, especially because the privileged Christians have been crying 'Don't mix politics with religion' when some Christian leaders tried to condemn the evils of apartheid. These privileged Christians have helped to perpetuate the myth that Christianity is just something one does on Sunday, and has nothing to do with ones rent or housing or unemployment.

The credibility of the Gospel is at stake. We, the Church of God, can redeem ourselves if we are determined to work together as the Churches in Ulster, to witness together against injustice and oppression and exploitation, to stand together with the poor and the oppressed throughout the world, and here in South Africa with the victims of one of the most ruthless systems in the world. The credibility of the Gospel may be restored if we become the voice of the voiceless. God be praised that during the recent unrest in the schools, our Churches were seen to stand by the children, to act with them and on their behalf. To do this and all the other things I have suggested, is going to be costly. I fear that this government in South Africa is becoming more authoritarian, and that it will tolerate criticism and dissent less and less. Christian leaders who stand up to be counted in the struggle for justice, are going to get it in the neck. They will be harassed, they will be detained and arrested, they will be banned, and some will die mysteriously in detention. Many will just disappear from the face of the earth, as has happened in Russia, in the Iron Curtain countries, in Nazi Germany, in Amin's Uganda.

But we have no option, because we serve Him who said of himself:

> 'The Spirit of the Lord is upon me,
> Because he has chosen me to bring
> Good news to the poor.
> He has sent me to proclaim liberty to the captives
> and recovery of sight to the blind,

118

To set free the oppressed
And announce that the time has come
When the Lord will save his people.'

41. Women and the Church

Bishop Tutu here supports the growing movement that is campaigning for a balanced priesthood.

I BELIEVE we are, as male and female, an example of the interdependence of being human. The self-sufficient human person is in many ways sub-human. In Africa we say 'A person is a person through others'—one's humanity is interwoven with that of others. I believe that males and females have distinctive gifts, and both sets of gifts are indispensable for truly human existence. I am sure the Church has lost something valuable in denying ordination to women for so long. There is something uniquely valuable that women and men bring to the ordained ministry, and it has been distorted and defective as long as women have been debarred. Somehow men have been less human for this loss. But I would like to stress that women priests must not be tempted to emulate men priests. There will be many things where your sex will be an irrelevance in carrying out your ministry as an ordained person; but there are many other occasions when peculiarly feminine insights will be your unique and distinctive contribution. That is why I am myself unhappy that women priests dress like men priests with dog collars. I know they have to assert that their priesthood is equal to that of men in all respects. But I would hope that they very quickly assert their self-assurance, and be women, not faint copies of men. They must not apologise for their existence, but celebrate their identity and personhood as women. That is what human liberation is all about. The Church and God's world need you as you, with your gentleness, your graciousness, your compassion.

There is something in the nature of God which corresponds to our maleness and our femaleness. We have tended to speak much more of the maleness, so we refer to the Fatherhood of God, which is as it should be. But we have missed out on the fullness that is God, when we have ignored that which corresponds to our femaleness. We have hardly spoken about the Motherhood of God, and consequently we have been the poorer for this.

I would like to refer to one aspect—a tremendous quality that women have—which relates to a like quality in God. It is the faith women have in people. Take a child who is a cause of much frustration and disillusion in others. The mother of that child can see the beauty and goodness hidden deep down, and women are much more patient than men in trying to bring that goodness to the surface. They have the capacity, more than men, to cherish that good and bring it to fruition. They are like the sculptor who can see the beautiful sculpture in a block of stone.

I think that is how God is—he has extraordinary patience with each one of us and sees us as we shall be. He brings to the surface the good that is hidden way down there and nurtures it, nurses it until it comes to full bloom. In many ways the manner in which Jesus handled Peter after the resurrection, is the way only God or a woman would. Peter, who had announced that he would follow Jesus to death, had not only denied Him thrice, but had fled and abandoned Him at the crucifixion. So he must have dreaded meeting Jesus after the resurrection. But notice the gentleness of Jesus. He asks Peter three times to declare he loves him, and three times gives him special responsibility—to cancel his threefold denial. That was believing in someone—affirming him so that he could have faith in himself.

Women, we need you to give us back our faith in humanity.

42. Children's Rights

From an address given at a Home and Family Life Conference, at Hammanskraal during the Year of the Child, on 2 March 1979.

MY WIFE and I decided early on in our marriage, that we were going to try to let our children do a lot of things that we had been denied in our childhood. We had been brought up to know that children are meant to be seen and not heard. So as children we used to feel so terribly frustrated when those gods in our household— our parents and their grown-up friends—were discussing something really interesting. We were burning to ask 'who or what' in order to clarify some obscure point, but we never dared to interrupt.

I remember we were often warned not even to *look* at grown-ups as they were involved in some animated conversation. Living in cramped quarters, it was practically impossible to be interested in ones books, whilst people were laughing and joking in the same room. We were told to leave the room when other grown-ups came to visit our demigods, and we had to be quick about producing the tea (at any old hour), which the 'gods' enjoyed guzzling in enormous quantities. We had to be content with surreptitious swigs at the small hole in the condensed milk tin when no one was looking.

So we thought we did not want our children to go through all those traumas. Perhaps it was reinforced by the fact that we had moved to England, where our antiquated methods were things of the distant and hoary past. But it was not easy. I remember for instance saying to our youngest, who was then a very chirpy three-year-old, and quite sure that there were very few things that she did not know in the world: 'Mpho, darling, please keep quiet, you talk too much!' Do you think she was at all deflated by this rebuke? Not at all—quick as a shot she retorted: 'Daddy, you talk a lot too. You talk all by yourself in Church!' Well I never. One should not make light of what is called Culture Shock, for it is very real. There we were, Leah and I, utterly conditioned by our upbringing not to be sassy and talk back at adults, whilst our children were in a culture where that is as normal as drinking tea. We were experiencing a new kind of trauma.

We stuck it out very painfully. We let them join in discussions with out adult friends—they interrupted, they argued, they contributed. I can tell you though, how we sometimes fumed, because one of our children had said: 'Oh Daddy, that's nonsense.' But we began to find that we had to relate to them as real persons, with points of view that had to be taken seriously. It was not enough to pull rank, and think it would suffice to say 'Do this.' 'Why?' they would ask. We had to begin to marshall facts to justify our position, not being merely authoritarian, although this might have made life less hectic from time to time.

Despite the traumas of belonging to two cultures, we know it was right to adopt the line we did. Children are a wonderful gift, and they are young and small persons, with minds and ideas, hating to be talked down at. They have an extraordinary capacity to see into the heart of things, and to expose sham and humbug for what they are. We must not idealise them too much, but I know that most of those I have had any dealings with respond wonderfully to being treated with respect, as persons who are responsible. There is the old saying: 'Give a dog a bad name and hang him.' If we treat our children as unreliable and dishonest why should we be surprised when they in fact behave as we reckon they would?

We are talking so much about liberation, about a just and participatory society, where decisions are not rammed down people's throats. We resent it, and quite rightly so, when people are forever letting us know what is good for us, when they are patronising or don't allow us to enjoy rights which we believe are inalienable, and which go with being human. But then in the society where we *can* do something about it, the home and family, we are a replica of the very society we condemn so roundly.

We discovered there was much fun in the home, and we parents developed as we pitted our strengths against those of our children.

They were persons in their own right, and we had to think out many things that previously we had taken for granted. It did not mean letting go of discipline, because a rebellious child is really testing out the parameters of acceptable conduct, and that is part of the painful process of growing up. And to have no standards that the family recognises, eventually means the child has nothing to test themselves against. Pandering to him/her in the end turns out to be the worst thing you could do for them, and they will resent it for the rest of their lives, that you failed to help them grow up responsibly. After all, they were trying to get away from being known as the child of so-and-so. They were looking for self-esteem and self-identity. We know how much we hate as blacks and maybe as women (black and white) to have our identity determined in terms of another.

Let us work positively, so that we can contribute to the recognition of Children's Rights, and thereby work for a more just and equitable society, where everybody will have the right to a full life, to a stable family existence, to a free and compulsory education, to freedom of movement and association, to freedom from ignorance, hunger, and fear, and freedom of thought and worship.

43. Into the Eighties

A press statement, released on 30 October 1979.

THE 1970s have been a decade of hope and despair. Hope because there has been so much concern about human freedom and rights around the world. Anyone flouting accepted standards of human rights could not do so with impunity. The whole world would be opposed to them. Much has been achieved in removing discrimination based on sex, colour, race and religion. But it has been a decade which has also seen people like Amin, Bokassa and others. There has been the ghastly spectacle of man's inhumanity to man in the Middle East, in the Far East, in Africa. We have seen a horrible increase in refugees the world over—in an affluent world there has been abject poverty and starvation, exploitation and oppression. But we believe it is God's world, and that one day His will for all of us will prevail. And so we go into the 1980s with a quiet confidence and optimism.

Bibliography

SOUTH AFRICA:

No easy walk to Freedom. Articles, speeches and trial addresses of Nelson Mandela. Edited by Ruth First. Heinemann 1980.

I write what I like. Steve Biko. A selection of his writings edited by Aelred Stubbs CR. Heinemann 1979.

Steve Biko. A biography by Donald Woods. Paddington Press 1978.

The Sun will Rise. Statements from the dock by South African political prisoners (including Robert Sobukwe and Nelson Mandela). Edited by Mary Benson. International Defence and Aid Fund, 1976.

The Church Struggle for Justice in South Africa. J. W. de Grouchy, SPCK 1979.

The Freedom Charter of South Africa 1955. Published by the United Nations Centre against Apartheid.

MISCELLANEOUS:

Profile of Love. Peter Mattheson. Christian Journals Ltd, Belfast 1979. Contains interesting assessments of the South African and Northern Ireland situations.

Mass Production or Production by the Masses? George McRobie and Marilyn Carr. Intermediate Technology Development Group 1977. London.

The Masque of Anarchy. P. B. Shelley 1819. Shelley's classic poem, written in the immediate aftermath of the Peterloo Massacre, deals with the great questions of oppression, protest, and freedom.